Psychology Revivals

Commonsense Psychology and the Home

First published in 1933, *Commonsense Psychology and the Home* was a book for parents and others who were interested in the welfare of the child and who, although sceptical of, and confused by, the conflicting schools of modern psychology at the time, desired guidance from modern knowledge combined with experience which they could appreciate as appealing to their common sense. It deals with the ideals of home life, from the choice of the partner to make a home, through the whole development of the family, ending up on the arrival of grandchildren. It shows the commonsense application of psychological principles to the happy and harmonious development of the home and the ultimate achievement of a freed personality when the child goes out into the world. It shows, step by step, how major difficulties may be avoided and minor difficulties handled.

This book is a re-issue originally published in 1933. The language used and views portrayed are a reflection of its era and no offence is meant by the Publishers to any reader by this re-publication.

Commonsense Psychology and the Home

Frederick H. Dodd

Routledge
Taylor & Francis Group
LONDON AND NEW YORK

First published in 1933
by George Allen & Unwin Ltd

This edition first published in 2025 by Routledge
4 Park Square, Milton Park, Abingdon, Oxon, OX14 4RN

and by Routledge
605 Third Avenue, New York, NY 10017

Routledge is an imprint of the Taylor & Francis Group, an informa business

A Library of Congress record exists under LCCN: 35000837

ISBN: 978-1-032-93881-3 (hbk)
ISBN: 978-1-003-56805-6 (ebk)
ISBN: 978-1-032-93884-4 (pbk)

Book DOI 10.4324/9781003568056

COMMONSENSE PSYCHOLOGY AND THE HOME

by

FREDERICK H. DODD, M.R.C.S. Eng., L.R.C.P. Lond.

Physician with charge of Department of Diseases of Children
and Children's Psychological Department,
Eastern Dispensary

Late Physician, Children's Department,
Tavistock Psychotherapeutic Clinic

LONDON
GEORGE ALLEN & UNWIN LTD
MUSEUM STREET

FIRST PUBLISHED IN 1933

PRINTED IN GREAT BRITAIN BY
UNWIN BROTHERS LTD., WOKING

FOREWORD

There is no need for a prolonged preface to this book since its object and the reasons for its existence will be found in the first chapter. I want, however, to take this opportunity of expressing my great obligation to my wife for her devoted assistance as colleague and constructive critic.

F. H. D.

CONTENTS

COMMONSENSE PSYCHOLOGY AND THE HOME

CHAPTER I

EMANCIPATION OF PERSONALITY

PEOPLE may ask why, when so much has been written during the past few years on the subject of child psychology, yet another book should be added. The answer is, that this book is primarily intended for parents, teachers and others who are busily engaged in the time-absorbing activities of child care. Such people, although they are tackling the practical problems, have little time to read and sift the varied literature describing the many schools of modern psychology. Students may do this, and will draw their own conclusions as to the valuable points set forward by the different leaders, but they are lacking in a knowledge of the practical application of their discoveries. Each of the schools of thought has discovered some truth at least which has its bearing on the normal and healthy child, and although there may be much antagonism, truth which proves to be of practical value cannot be ignored, especially when it coincides with what we realize to be common sense. The subject-matter of this book sets out to be the combined result of both study and the practical experience of handling children over a period of some years.

There is obviously one great objection to the study of modern psychology in an endeavour to do the best for our normal healthy children. That is, it tends to attract our attention too much to what we think ought to happen, so that we are worried when our child appears to be deviating from what we imagine should be its normal development. However, look at a corresponding situation on a physical plane. Let us suppose that we have no knowledge of First Aid, or of the Science of Anatomy or Physiology. Under such circumstances we should allow our children to grow up under conditions which they might survive, but which would inevitably fall far short of the best. We might keep them in stuffy, unventilated rooms because the day was cold. We should not know how to deal with their minor accidents, and so forth. If, on the other hand, we had a full knowledge of these subjects, there would be a danger of our trying to establish such perfection in their hygienic conditions that, the moment they were exposed to any less satisfactory surroundings, they would fall victims to the first disease with which they came in contact. We might be so much frightened of the possible consequences of injury that we should refuse to allow our children to take part in the normal rough and tumble of life. It is, however, possible to add to our technical knowledge of these matters a realization of the importance of a free and natural development of the child, so establishing a healthy balance between hygienic surroundings and a normal and unrestricted life, secure in the knowledge that if illness or accident did occur we should be in the best possible position to deal with it. In fact, we should recognize the earliest signs of disease and so avert a more serious development thereof by simple expedients. In the same way, a knowledge of the essentials of modern psychology in relation to the emotional development of our children will prove of the utmost value, provided it is used as a precaution and not as overcaution. Every child is, of course, liable to mild psychological disorders, just as it is to physical disorders. They both need treatment, which is obviously best given as early, and with as much understanding, as possible. Emotional difficulties, taken in the early stages, might be likened to a tangled skein of wool, which would resolve itself into a simple, straight thread by a deft shake of the hand. This same tangle, if left or dealt with clumsily, might tie itself into an irrevocable knot, thus leaving a perpetual tangle or, at the best, a broken thread which will of necessity weaken the final woven fabric.

It is remarkable how many people of adult years, and leading apparently normal lives, are actually suffering from limitations or, perhaps, more serious disabilities, which could have been entirely avoided had early adjustments been more knowledgeably handled.

Amongst those who are sceptical of the psychological point of view, one tends, broadly speaking, to find two types. Firstly, there are those who see clearly in their own minds what they want their children to be and do. Such people obviously mutilate the personality of their children by their own dominance. We all recognize this when we see it in its obvious dictatorial form, but nowadays there are many children who suffer equally from this same over-shadowing which is expressed more subtly. Think of the parents who, with the best intention in the world, let their children know they will never tell them to act in a certain way, but who at the same time lovingly let their children realize that any action which deviates from the parental point of view will pain them deeply.

The other type are the more happy-go-lucky parents, who generously feel they will give the children a good time while they are young; life is hard—let the little ones enjoy themselves. So they, figuratively speaking, pack their family into a coach and say: "Drive about and enjoy yourselves. You are good, you are young, you will arrive somewhere." And later, they are disappointed and hurt that the children have not driven up successfully to the door of adulthood, and the children turn round and ask their parents where they have landed them, and why; and they start out in their larger life bewildered and embittered. In the first half of this book it will be well, therefore, to try to focus in a generalized way those things towards which we are guiding the child.

Another reason for taking these wider aspects first is a renewed emphasis on the fact that our own attitude of mind, and our own emotional reactions, have more bearing on the child than any amount of teaching, so that although much of the earlier chapters may appear remote from the subject of child psychology, it is really far more closely allied with it than would appear at first sight.

It is an interesting experiment to see what ideas first come into one's mind when one thinks of the word "adulthood." After this it may be interesting to carry out similar experiments with such words as "love," "friendship," "childhood," "responsibility" and "work." It is more than likely we shall find that our first idea concerning each of these words is by no means what we feel to be ideal, and we shall want to find out why we have developed such polarized ideas concerning these concepts. Undoubtedly they have been developed during our early years.

Having accepted the fact that our point of view has to some extent been warped by various emotional stimuli in the past, let us shut our eyes to this and look afresh, and reconsider what we mean by adulthood. Certainly it is not just the achievement of adult years, stature or intelligence. May we not define it as the arrival at a state of true harmony of our powers and instincts, this being based on our innate capacity, expressing itself in an independent personality, capable of handling to the best advantage any environment in which it may be placed; a state in which we are subservient to no authority other than that which we believe to be right? There are many people with a high grade of intelligence, of excellent physique, of very mature years, who are yet, in essential respects, still children dominated by authority, tied down by fears and who are still emotionally in a state of dependence. Peter Pan in real life is a tragedy.

These immature personalities may be fortunate enough to get materially established in life with apparent success, but they are not capable of taking their part, in a full and healthy way, in their contact with others, and they have, of course, to find the road to freedom themselves. If this is so, how can they show the road to their children? Not only will their blindness prevent them from leading the next generation along the right road, but fear will make them put obstacles in the way should the children discover the road for themselves. There are many complex psychological situations which may prevent the attainment of emotional maturity, but there is one straightforward factor which has an immense bearing on this question. That is, a realization that our attitude to death affects our attitude to life. The difficulty which people have in passing harmoniously into middle age or old age is fundamentally connected with this. Because the majority of us are afraid of death we ignore the question, both in our own lives and in the upbringing of our children. One tends to avoid the subject of death with a child or, if it is raised by the child himself, it is often dealt with in a sepulchral and mysterious manner, whereas if from our early years we had a sense of the adventure into the unknown, which we must all of us some day experience, it would become interwoven with our general attitude to tackling life as an ever-unfolding adventure.

It often seems to be forgotten that childhood is a small part only of the whole life of the individual, and that it is of greater importance for the longer part to be happy. Not that childhood should not and cannot be happy, but we must always bear in mind that it is more vital for the child to grow up into a happy, harmonized adult than to be pleased with a momentary situation, when it would lead to greater ultimate happiness for it to be displeased for a brief space.

Towards what are we really trying to guide our children? Not just to make their mark in the world of fame or finance, or even of social service, but rather to enable them to grow to their fullest and freest extent along all the lines of their development—physical, emotional and intellectual. No two children, given precisely the same upbringing, will develop similarly. There is individuality even in the cell from which the child develops. Each cell has its own characteristics, its own developmental tendencies. Just as, on the physical plane, we find that the child which has tuberculosis in its family history will have a tendency towards tuberculosis, and that the child which has insanity in its family history will have a tendency towards mental instability (although in both cases this tendency can be dealt with effectively by suitable environmental handling), so also we have definite tendencies towards certain lines of capacity, and certain lines of weakness, in the emotional and intellectual spheres. We shall find also characteristics within these spheres which will definitely manifest themselves in the child. It is these characteristics which must be made use of in the child's life. All we should do is to free the child's own psyche and encourage the development of its best tendencies.

There has been of late a tendency to consider that if the best is given in the way of hygiene and education the same type of treatment should be suitable to all children. On the other hand, there has also been a tendency to take the line that the child can find its own way, and should not be interfered with by any form of discipline or guidance unless the child itself asks for such. In view of their lack of experience it is impossible to expect children always to ask for guidance when they need it, and the method of training by experience may carry them far from normal and healthy developmental lines.

During childhood and adolescence the individual's outlook may be diagramatically expressed by a horizontal line representing the present. He thinks and acts and bases his values of life essentially in the present, and comparatively little of importance is attached to the future or to the past. Gradually, however, there develops a vertical line. The horizontal line becomes limited while the vertical line becomes extended indefinitely in either direction; that is to say, into the past and into the future. An outlook on life is achieved, basing its values on a composite appreciation of the present in relation to the past and the future.

The establishment of this vertical line is an essential element of true adulthood, and is therefore one of

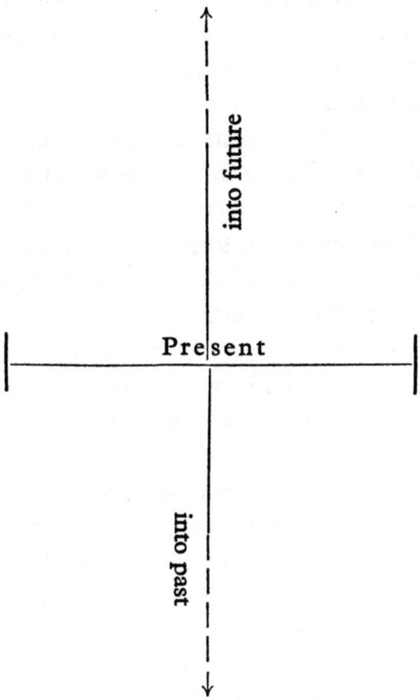

the fundamental principles of education. Before birth the human child goes through various evolutionary stages of animal life. Education consists largely in living through the various stages of man until we reach the full stature of present-day man. The child before the age of twelve years should be encouraged to live vividly in the past, to feel himself into the life of savages, of ancient Greeks and early mariners, etc. It is not until after this that the boy and girl should be deeply concerned with social problems. Social problems and ideals involve a vision of the future, a vision of the world as we should like it to be, and the child is not ready to consider life from this point of view unless its judgments are based on firm knowledge and sense-feeling of the past. One cannot, of course, pass straight on from the past to the future, so that education in the teens should include practical knowledge of the life of to-day; for example, political situations, national and international, visits to factories, and various other aspects of citizenship. At the age of seventeen or eighteen the development of the vertical line really begins to make itself evident. It coincides with the period of emergence from the limited world of home into the greater world outside the home. The transition stage from that of the horizontal line to the co-ordination of the horizontal and vertical components may be a really difficult period in the adolescent's life.

It has already been said that material success is not an index to true adulthood. In fact, concentration on material things tends to indicate restriction of the vertical component of our diagram, and it is only when we come to recognize the importance of personality as compared with material things that we come to satisfactory criteria for the estimation of adulthood, namely, the emancipation of personality. The essential thing in corporate social life is the interaction of adult personalities, which, being neither subordinate to nor in rebellion against any form of human authority, are therefore able to accept the dictates of their own judgment as to what is right in relation to the whole body of the society in which they live. Material things are of no value except so far as they are related to personality, which in its turn is of value so far as it is related to the common good. Much has been said of recent years about freedom of personality, but a great deal of this has tended to emphasize "I want" rather than "what is needed from me." This would be harmless if the two phrases were synonymous, as they should be, but unfortunately they too often tend to be antagonistic.

The small child feels that it should be able to gratify every self-centred desire. Ere long, however, it discovers that it cannot take with impunity as many biscuits as it wants. The child fears disapproval and will do anything in its power to gain the approval of its parents or others representing them. In the final and adult stage it becomes altruistic and will do anything for the benefit of others, even though such action may never be recognized.

At this point we may perhaps amplify our definition of "full adulthood." We see that it involves facing facts with wide-open eyes, and facing hard facts with knowledgeable bravery but not blind recklessness; and that it acknowledges a standard of ideals based on the judgment of right and wrong and not on outside opinion. The fully developed adult welcomes responsibility and would rather support than cling, so friendships are based on interchange of experience rather than on mutual interdependence. The true adult may be regarded as a complete entity, prepared to take either his or her place, neither more nor less, in the corporate structure of society.

CHAPTER II

MARRIAGE AND CREATIVE FORCE

THERE is nothing which gives a greater sense of pleasure and satisfaction than achievement in creation. This is evident right through life. The tiny child or the baby which balances a few bricks and calls it a train or a car glows with delight at its power of creation. Our judgment of work is based on a realization of the joy in creation. We term work which repeats the same process day after day menial and uninteresting, but wherever there is a chance of initiative and scope for the creative impulse of the person working, we look upon that work as satisfactory and happy. Robert Bridges was expressing the fundamental urge of every living personality in the lines:

> I, too, will something make, and joy in the making,
> E'en though to-morrow it seem
> Like the empty days of a dream
> Remembered on waking.

Here you have a description of that urge to create, quite irrespective of whether that which is being created will last or not. Sex, as applying to the physical relationships and contacts between human beings, is only part of this strong creative urge. That is why the sex instinct, when expressed physically with no creative purpose, leads to dissatisfaction, depression and loss of energy. This does not mean that physical sex is only satisfied in relation to the creation of a child, but it does mean that it is unsatisfactory when it is purely on a physical plane. Behind the normal, healthy, happy marriage there is a desire to create a home, to create children and to give some joint adult contribution to the world. If all these three elements are missing, as is sometimes the case, it is safe to say that the marriage is eventually doomed to failure. That is to say, when two people marry, with the idea that they will be all in all to each other, they look no farther than this. An inevitable factor in the human make-up has been denied expression. It is perfectly natural that some economic factors render it in many cases impossible, or at any rate undesirable, that there should be large families. Woman, to be happy, must have a further outlet for her creative energy, to compensate for her restricted maternal creativeness; otherwise she will tend to over-mother and over-fuss such children as she has, and will feel thwarted and irritated with the daily duties of everyday life. The joint creativeness in work makes for a far happier marital relationship than the use of contraceptives. You may ask what all this has to do with the upbringing of children. The answer is twofold. Firstly, the training of children in matters concerning sex is one of the most important factors in education, because, being such a powerful force, it has more bearing all through life on real health and happiness, both mental and physical, than has anything else. Secondly, the relationship of the father and mother to each other and to the child is of paramount importance. However much modern teaching may try to convince us that home influence is negligible, or even bad, and that the father is merely an instrument in the creation of the child, and that motherhood is simply a biological consummation of womanhood, it is evident in dealing with numbers of cases of mental instability, depression, illness and crime, that failure in the home relationships is a vitally important factor. It has been said by many psychologists that if there were no broken homes there would be no split personalities. It is certainly true that a broken home inevitably scars the personality of the child, although there are other factors which may cause the same type of difficulty, such as disagreement in authority between the parents and the grandparents if they both exercise authority over the child, or even conflict between the home and the school may have really serious effects. If, then, the home relationship is so vital a factor in the upbringing of the child, it may be well to go into some of the factors which affect this background. It will also be evident that the preparation for ultimate marriage is involved in the experiences of the child in its own home.

Much thought has been given in recent years to the training of children in matters of sex, but it is quite evident that this cannot be rightly handled in an isolated manner. The parents' own unspoken attitude probably has quite as much bearing on the training of the child as has any careful educational process, so that in order to get things into true focus we shall have to review the past, namely, the parents' basis of marriage, the present, the child's own sex development, and thirdly, as clear a view as possible of the psychologically sound adult attitude to marriage and sex.

Looking at the matter in this way we become involved in a continuous spiral of thought, as it were, winding its way on into the future, and it is difficult to see from which point it is best to start to get the clearest view.

It is usual to take the line that the child has life before it, and that therefore if we deal soundly with sex education in childhood all will be well; but surely it is wiser for the parents first to review the basis of their own marriage and their own attitude to sex, in this way gaining a background of psychological honesty to all their future training. There is nothing more dangerous than insincerity in dealing with sex matters. Discovery of falsehood or insincerity by the child on the part of the parents is one of the commonest causes of behaviour-difficulties and crime.

When we come to consider the types of marriage which take place, we find a large number in which love was misinterpreted and in which infatuation has been regarded as synonymous to love.

The origin of infatuation is physical, and is often based on some previous emotional situation. It is therefore important to guard against misinterpreting infatuation, from whatever cause it may arise, as the love required for a true united marriage. It is obvious that a marriage of purely physical infatuation would not be satisfactory. Attraction on intellectual, ethical and physical planes is essential for true comradeship.

It may be helpful to consider successful marriage under the heading of three types, the most fruitful of which, though perhaps the most difficult of adjustment, is the marriage of opposites. It is obvious that such partners will bring entirely different contributions to their marriage. There will be innumerable points where their mode of approach will be different, and they will tend to hold divergent opinions on many subjects. A keen sense of the real value of the other's personality, an honest meeting at every point of difficulty, a willingness to give each other freedom to approach problems from his or her own angle, may lead to an amalgamation which will greatly increase their joint power of service in the world.

It is not just $a + b$, but ab. Just as these two symbols become more closely united to form a product, so the unity of marriage gives the product, rather than the sum, of the two individual capacities; further, this product becomes of greater value than the sum, as the individual values of a and b are increased.

Another type of marriage, easier to work out, but by no means having such great potentialities, is the marriage of similar types. Such a marriage will obviously involve only minor points of disagreement to be solved, and there will be little resultant widening of outlook and clarifying of vision.

The third type of marriage is that in which one partner is of the dominant type and the other of the submissive. Such a marriage may be quite happy, although there is always a danger that the situation may become one of imperceptible but steady increase in dominance on the part of the one partner and submissiveness on the part of the other, with a steady decrease in the value to others of their united life and a gradual development of unhappiness in the home.

The problem of the person of adult years, but not emotionally mature, has already been mentioned. For instance, an immature man may tend to seek in his mate a mother rather than a wife, and so will marry a girl whose instincts are more maternal than wifely, and who is usually older than himself. The arrival of a child in a marriage such as this may cause untold difficulty, because the husband, who had sought the comfort of a devoted mother, resents the appearance of a rival. He becomes jealous of his own child, and, in extreme cases, possibly vindictive towards the child's mother for having failed to give him what he had expected in his married life.

The reverse situation is also comparatively common, namely, that of a man with a strong paternal instinct marrying a girl much younger than himself, really seeking a daughter rather than a wife. In such a marriage there is real danger that the girl may meet another man who could really be her comrade and with whom marriage could be a real thing, and so unhappiness may follow. Similarly, in the case of the immature man who has married his mother: he may develop farther with his new maternal guidance and contacts in the outside world, and so grow to a capacity for true marriage and really fall in love with someone other than his wife.

These mother-son and father-daughter marriages are frequently examples of the dominant-submissive partnerships. Such marriages do not, of course, invariably turn out complete failures, but in order that there should be an appreciable measure of success the situation must be accepted knowingly by both partners.

This is but a brief consideration of types of marriage. There are one or two tests which are invaluable in determining the nature of the relationship which those concerned interpret as love. It is evident that there must be a physical attraction. This sounds obvious, but there are cases where young people imagine themselves to be in love in spite of the absence of such attraction. There must also be a sense of intellectual affinity: there must be genuine interest and power to participate in the other's interests, even though they may never have thought of them before. Last, but by no means least, is the importance of what may be called ethical affinity. The only test for this is the power to find the greatest happiness in free discussion of the deepest things in each other's lives. It is on this last ground that the unhappiness of so many marriages is founded. It is surprising how often two people, who consider themselves really in love, have never attempted, still less achieved, entry into the holy of holies in each other.

Assuming that two people have chosen rightly to enter upon the great adventure of marriage, it is necessary that they should consider, as far as possible, the general principles which must guide them in this adventure. They must not go blindly forward with the idea that it is impossible to foresee what this new life will mean. It is true that it cannot be foreseen in detail, but there are certain principles which can be appreciated as important, and adherence to which may save many pitfalls.

Successful marriage is more than comradeship. It involves an emotional and intellectual unity, symbolized by a complete physical unity. The sooner the implications of this unity are faced, the happier the marriage. The general principle involved may be best summarized in the following statement: that all past relationships with both relatives and friends must be severed, and instead a new relationship, in which the husband and wife are accepted as one, must be developed. Nothing can be more fatal to happiness in marriage than independent relationships with other people. This does not mean that the husband and wife must always be together, nor that one may not meet people whom the other never sees, but it does mean that there is a constant sense of the one partner in the other partner's life. It means a constant acceptance of their unity, both by themselves and by their friends and relatives, and the recognition of this unity in all other relationships into which they may enter. For this reason it is essential that the physical consummation of marriage should not be delayed, since the lack of symbolism of physical unity leaves a sense of incompleteness on other planes. The failure of satisfaction of the instinctive physical demands may give rise to serious stresses and emotional depression often expressed in irritability and antagonism.

There is a danger of married people confusing unity of the face-to-face variety, in which there is complete satisfaction of the needs of the one by the other, with the unity of the side-by-side type, which involves two people unitedly looking out upon the world, and so taking their part as one, to greater effect than the sum of their individual powers would have rendered possible. Quite apart from the obvious social importance of this latter attitude, it is only by this means that parents will help their children to realize the importance of the development of a right attitude towards society. What the parents do and are is the most important factor in the development of ideals in their children.

The small child, from the very beginning of its life, is demanding the mother as its essential need, and the father is a power which takes the mother from the child. From this point of view the child is up against the father and jealous of his relation to the mother. It is clear that if there is any lack of unity between the parents (and such a lack of unity is very easily detected by the child however careful the parents may be to hide it) there will be encouragement for the child to express its jealousy, with undesirable results. If, on the other hand, the child has a sense of the complete unity of the parents, its jealousy of the father will tend to die a natural death, since it can find no means of effective expression. In order to ensure this satisfactory development, it is necessary that the father should obviously need the mother, and should identify himself with her in relation to their child. He should also from the very beginning establish a sense of his deep interest and love for it, and should give it the opportunity for steady development and understanding of him and what he stands for, which will gradually and normally pass over into a phase of hero-worship for the father which will later be described.

It is important, too, that the mother should realize this question of jealousy, and should counter this by emphasizing her whole attitude towards her husband, her unity with and affection for him. Whatever line she takes with regard to him is likely to be adopted by her child.

Before being ready to deal with the direct method of handling the question of early sex training and instinct in the child, it is exceedingly helpful to test ourselves by thinking of the word "sex" and the phrase "creative force." How many of us could honestly say that the word "sex" was not polarized for us, and that unpleasantly, as compared with the phrase "creative force"?

"Sex" is a word which is interpreted in many ways by different people, and is perhaps one of the most polarized words in the English language. It is the most repressed of all our instincts as the result of the conventions of civilization. There is no serious stigma attached to the person who loses his temper or is afraid on some occasion, but this tends not to be the case where a fall from grace involves the sex instinct. At present there is a superficial tendency to condone such lapses, and even to attempt to justify them, but deep down there is still, and always will be, a sense of guilt and stigma attached to them. Far beyond control exercised by convention is the sense of taboo only too often imposed by parents and others in charge of children. This may lead children to rebellion, and so they deal crudely with such matters, and there arises a sense of guilt and impurity in connection with the word "sex." This is one reason for the suggestion of the term "creative force" in the title of this chapter. Another reason, however, is this: "sex" definitely suggests a limited meaning as applying to physical relations and contacts between human beings, whereas "creative force" expresses a far wider application of the same instinct in the whole conduct of life. In everyone there is a desire to create; primarily, of course, there is the desire for physical intercourse between man and woman, which may lead to the birth of a child and the release of direct creative instinct in parenthood. As a result of unsatisfactory initiation into the whole subject, a great many people are up against serious difficulties with regard to the healthy and happy acceptance of these instincts on the physical plane. Nevertheless, if we try to depolarize our ideas, even though emotionally we may not be able to get quite clear, we shall see logically that it ought to be possible for us to recognize that the physical processes involved are wonderful. If we are unable to accept this wholeheartedly the fault lies in ourselves and not in the processes. Whatever, then, our own emotional feeling may be, we shall see that it is of vital importance to our children that they should be saved as far as possible from an unhealthy and repressive attitude towards sex.

The question of creative expression outside marriage is an independent problem, but it may be asked how this instinct, if it is not to be directly expressed on the physical plane, is to be dealt with in the unmarried. The reply to this is that it is by no means completely expressed even in marriage, and that if it were, married people would automatically become useless members of the community, except for the value of their contribution in children. Even when our children have been born, our creative part in relation to them is by no means over, since it is still our function, by leading and guiding their development, to help in the ultimate creation of a healthy and freed adult. True, in this process our attitude must be objective creativeness, not subjective self-expression. We must help the child to express itself rather than try to mould it into a model of what we should like it to be, for if we did this we should merely be expressing ourselves, and we should be irritated and might even dislike our children if they departed from our self-created standard.

All who have to deal with children have their creative part to play. The child's nurse, the school teacher, the matron of the convalescent home or orphanage, the doctor and the clergyman, can all express their creativeness in this way. These would all be satisfying their creative urge, inasmuch as they were responsible for influencing the child along any definite line.

Creative urge can, of course, find expression in methods other than those involved in direct human contact. The architect and the engineer, for example, are expressing directly their creative instinct, but in nearly all forms of work this instinct is manifesting itself to a greater or lesser degree.

In the same way, these natural instincts are expressed in the normal play-life of the child, either consciously or unconsciously. The little girl playing quietly with her dolls is expressing directly her desire for motherhood. The small boy, with his hammer, nails and wood, may have a vivid conscious thrill in his creative power as he hammers away making a play liner. The very games and work of the child derive their energy from the spring provided by the primitive instincts. It is of vital importance to realize this in order that we may avoid repression, since repression of primitive urges does not destroy those urges, but means that they must needs find expression in some other way which may not be nearly so desirable as the original outlet devised by the child. We may often be tempted to prevent the child from doing something which strikes us as unsound from an adult standpoint, whereas if we stopped for a moment to see through the child's eyes we should realize that it is a perfectly normal and healthy occupation. If, however, as may happen, the child's mode of outlet is *really* unsound, repression is still the wrong mode of approach. Some other similar and socially accepted outlet must be found.

To give a very vivid example: there is the story of a little boy who found great pleasure in wetting things with his urine and found that he attracted the attention of other children by making fountains. He was cured by being encouraged to hose the garden, which was much more fun as the fountain produced was far larger.

Little boys who do such things are so often treated as if they were nasty-minded, or were doing something really wrong, when the unpleasant aspect may be only in the mind of the adult. To the child at the outset such action may be merely the expression of power. Such behaviour as this, wisely handled, may pass off with perfect ease into other satisfactory outlets, but if handled wrongly the sense of guilt and impurity will inevitably be built into the child's character.

Apart from the free expression of the normal creative instinct, the child will also seek knowledge about the practical facts of physical sex. Children will almost invariably ask questions concerning sex, in some form or other, during the first four or five years of life. Such questions must be answered with truth as fully as the child needs. This last qualification, "as fully as the child needs," is a very important one. The emphasis should be laid on the fact that what the child is told must be the truth, but it need not, and should not, be the whole truth. When the child asks, "Where do babies come from?" one child may be satisfied with the answer, "God sends them"; another child will ask, "But how?" Obviously the second child will lead on to a more detailed discussion, such as that of sowing the seeds and the growth of plants, and the sowing of seed babies and the growth of babies. The soft warm covering of the chestnut may be a very suitable simile for the way the child is kept warm within its mother.

The objection may be raised that if we tell children about such things early, there is a danger of their indiscriminately passing on their knowledge to other children, and possibly causing themselves to be misjudged. This fear is groundless, since the whole sex question is so deeply rooted in the sacred in the history of the race, that it is easy to establish a situation in which the child looks upon all such knowledge as a sacred bond between itself and its parents. Thus is laid the foundation of an intimate confidence between parents and child which will spread into all the future relationships and experiences of the child's life.

If such knowledge as is given to the child in its early years is really carefully given, in just such quantity as the child can comfortably absorb, the whole matter of sex will slip into place as part of its general acceptance of life as a whole.

Sex matters will then probably lie quiescent until adolescence, when the whole problem will need to be explained in a more detailed and adult way.

CHAPTER III

AUTHORITY AND DISCIPLINE

WHEN considering the question of discipline and authority, it is of value to consider the exact nature of the influence which the parents and others have over the child, as well as the influence of inherited tendencies.

Education essentially must be a drawing out and developing of the child's own personality, rather than an impression of the adult on the child. Although probably almost everyone would accept this fact in theory, it is not so easy to carry out in practice. Only too often we try to impress our own adult views on the child, and so distort its normal development. This is one of the most important reasons why children grow up to take a line in life which is often diametrically opposed to the views of their parents.

The child's normal urge is towards its own greatest efficiency, and it will naturally want to find expression for its primitive instincts. These instincts are in themselves *amoral*, and it is the guiding of these along socially acceptable lines which constitutes education; so education in the various peoples of mankind differs according to the accepted social code of each nation.

At first the child will just make self-centred demands for expression of its primitive urges. Gradually the social sense will develop, until, in ideal adulthood, complete harmony should be achieved. It is the conflict between the primitive and the socially accepted which constitutes the difficulty in adjustment to life. The most important period from this point of view is the first five or six years of life. It may safely be said that if a child has learnt to adapt successfully to the changes of environment during these years it will require exceptional strain later to break down this developing harmony.

It will not be difficult, perhaps, to form a fairly clear opinion as to the way in which the tiny child is learning to adapt to constant minor changes in its surroundings. There are, however, likely to be two big tests of this adaptation:

(1) The arrival of another child in the family, and
(2) The early adaptation to school life.

The latter will be dealt with more fully in a subsequent chapter, but as the reaction following the arrival of a new child affects to some extent the basic principle of authority and discipline it will be well to consider it now.

Until the arrival of the new baby, the elder child, especially if up till then the only one, tends to constitute the first call on the mother's attention and affection. Then comes the baby, who necessarily absorbs the attention of the mother, and becomes to a great extent the centre of the picture. Although these facts form a valuable test of the child's progress, it is only right that the situation should be handled as understandingly as possible, so that not only is emotional shock avoided, but a right relationship between the child and its parents is encouraged.

It is really valuable to allow the child to know of the coming baby. No child need have a shock with regard to a new arrival. Some truthful preparation about its coming should be made. The tiniest child can understand something. It is important that the new baby should be introduced into the home as the joint possession of the whole family. This may be done in many ways, but it is often useful for the parents and the older child or children to be together, and for the new child to be brought in to them. Consider for a moment the feelings of a little two or three-year-old who has had no previous preparation when it is taken into its mother's room and sees a new little baby warmly snuggled up against Mother. It is expected to welcome this new little brother or sister with joy, yet it sees it for the first time usurping the position which hitherto the older child has considered its own special privilege.

It is said advisedly, "it is often useful for the *parents* to be with the older child under such circumstances" rather than just "for the mother and older child" to be together, because the linking of the *father* with the mother in the child's mind at such a period of emotional adjustment is particularly valuable, and has its bearing on the question of future authority and discipline.

In considering the question of the underlying psychological nature of authority and discipline and the right mode of their achievement, it must be clearly understood that there are two functions which inevitably enter into the relationship between the parents and the child. They are (1) love and (2) fear. So far as the problem of authority and discipline in early life is concerned, we must consider love and fear purely from a psychological point of view, though at the same time we must recognize that the interpretation of love required for this purpose falls far short of the full interpretation of the word as applied to ultimate human relationships.

Why is fear an essential factor? In the small child's early realization of the existence of the father in the family picture, it sees him as an all-powerful giant who can, and does, interfere with the child's possession of its mother. At the same time it also sees him as an all-powerful family protector. This double picture necessarily gives rise to two reactions. In the first place, the child is jealous and would like to overcome its dominant father. This gives rise to various mechanisms, such as getting equal to him, destroying him by magic, etc., as is shown in many of the popular fairy tales, such as *Jack and the Beanstalk* and *Jack the Giant Killer*. Identification with the father is another means of getting equal to him, and, as will be seen, is also an important factor in a child's development. The child feels that if the father knew what was going on in its mind he would punish it, and this is the genesis of the universal primitive fear of the father. At the same time, its feeling that the father is the all-powerful protector of itself and its mother induces the sense that the father is a loving father, and this realization calls for a correspondingly loving response from the child.

Just as we have a love factor due to the father's protective power, so, in relation to the mother, we have the love factor due to the fact that she supplies the child's needs and is the source of all its earliest satisfaction. At the beginning of its life the child does not distinguish between itself and its mother, but as it learns to do so this element of love remains a potent factor.

It is obvious that the small boy who plays with trains, soldiers, etc., is showing his masculine tendencies therein, while the little girl who prefers dolls is showing her maternal instinct. It is therefore not difficult to believe that these instincts will show themselves also in relationships with the parents, and that while children of both sexes will have an attachment to the mother on account of their dependence on her, the small boy will have a special attachment to the mother, while the small girl will tend to have a special attachment to the father, and in this we have a further factor which may be included under the heading of love.

It will be evident that the boy will have a strong tendency to identify himself with his father, not only as standing for what he himself aspires to be as he gets older, but also as being in a position in which he can express his protective affection for the mother, while the small girl will tend to identify herself with her mother.

The development of these early factors can be indefinitely modified, for good or for bad, by the degree of parental unity. The earliest practical opportunity by which this unity can be emphasized is during the period of the child's early feeding, when it is suggested that the father should be freely present while the baby is being fed, but that others, if present at all, should only be occasional visitors.

In this way the child's earliest intimate relationship with its mother is insolubly united with the unity of mother and father. It is, however, useless to act a part in this respect, since no apparent unity will deceive the child when a cleavage really exists. If this unity is established in the child's mind it will identify one parent with the other, to such an extent that it will always tend to react to either parent as it would to both, from the point of view of authority and discipline.

It is also obvious that neither parent should exaggerate the sense of fear, but the emphasis should be on the sense of *love*. The element of fear will in any case carry out its function. But what is this function? It is the basis of the earliest development of "conscience." We shall assume the identification of the parents to have been successfully brought about. As has been pointed out, the child has a primitive fear of punishment by the father, hence it must do what the father wishes. On account of its identification with the father, it develops its early "conscience," whereby it feels a sense of guilt and consequent need for punishment for any breach of the criteria which it has set up, based on what it believes to be the will of the parents. The importance of the nature and extent of the limitations adopted by the child's own "conscience" from its estimate of the parents' will is enormous. Three things may happen. The whole attitude of the parents may have been such as to cut down the sense of fear and develop a sense of united love, and at the same time to impose as few restrictions as possible on the child's conduct. They may have utilized the love factors wherever possible at the expense of the fear factors. In such a case necessary limitations of conduct will probably have been not only few, but such as the child can itself understand and appreciate, and which fit in with its own criteria of conduct. Under these circumstances the child will still need the guidance of some external criteria on account of its lack of experience, but its personality will be developing as freely as is possible under the conditions of civilized society. As the child receives this guidance, it steadily takes advantage of its own experience, and develops to a greater or lesser extent an *independent* judgment of right and wrong. This should ultimately develop into a completely free psychological "conscience," resulting in a healthy, unrestricted adult life. This is the ideal for our children towards which we must strive.

If the limitations which the child has to adopt in its early "conscience" are excessive, and are associated too much with the fear, guilt and punishment syndrome, which has already been described, the child's normal urges will constantly be opposed to its "conscience." An internal conflict will be set up. It will never be able to express itself freely. It will be over-dominated by its parents and by others. If this conflict becomes too intense, the child's natural urges have to defy its "conscience." Resultant conduct will be unsatisfactory, and the child will appear naughty or rebellious, and sometimes outbreaks of serious anti-social conduct may take place. If we talk to the child about such behaviour it will generally say truthfully that it is sorry but that it could not help it. It will feel guilty and may even be unsatisfied unless it is punished. It may even punish itself. Of course this will only happen when rebellion is completed. While the outburst is still in progress the child will refuse to recognize the dictates of "conscience." Realization of this will often help us to understand why a child appears unrepentant, and why punishment at that point proves ineffective. Firmness will bring the rebellion to an end, but the important thing is that the firmness should be a support to the child and not an additional weight on an already overburdened "conscience." It will be found that once the rebellion is over the child will be prepared to talk out the whole situation with the parent or anyone else who is sufficiently understanding and will co-operate in any rightly motivated line of punishment which is going to be helpful.

This leads us to digress for a moment and consider the meaning of "punishment." Our first feeling is that punishment is a form of aggression, something whereby the older person is able to have his own back on the younger and weaker, a retaliation for some conduct on the part of the child which has irritated the grown-up. This is all wrong. Punishment should never mean this.

As there is so much discussion as to the rightness or wrongness of punishment, we must define what might be called right punishment. In its right meaning punishment is by no means aggressive. It is the imposition on the part of the child or others of some line of action which is directed towards strengthening the child's own "conscience" where it is necessary that it should be strengthened. It is a process which, in the case of the healthy child, can be talked over, and in which its willing co-operation can be obtained. This sense of co-operation is the most important factor in the carrying out of such discipline. Punishment along such lines gives the child a sense that it has "paid its bill," and acts as a reminder in the case of a similar situation arising in the future. When we find that much of such discipline is necessary we may suspect that the child's "conscience" is really over-filled with limitations. If this is the case the right line for us to take is to endeavour to guide the child to greater freedom of expression and to reduce the limitations. This can obviously best be done by those from whom the child has developed its original "conscience."

Apart from the question of excessive limitations,

the child may incorporate in its "conscience" a number of limitations for which it can see no reason, but which it has passively accepted on the authority of its parents. This situation causes not only undue internal conflict, but a limitation of the judgment of right and wrong.

For example, under certain conditions the child knows from experience that it should react in a certain way, but if these conditions are slightly changed it has no general principles of its own to guide it as to how to modify its reactions. Thus we get the child who wants routine and becomes disturbed and difficult if the routine is broken into; it can carry on quite well so long as it does not have to face any new moral problems, but at the slightest novelty appearing it is undecided and has to seek advice. Such a child must inevitably develop the indecision of character with which we so often meet, even in older people.

Having briefly worked out what we may call "psychological conscience," showing ideal development and factors which may change that development, it is only right to say that this must be regarded as the mental medium by which a far deeper innate sense of right may be expressed. We may roughly liken the individual to the typist, the typewriter and the typewritten material. The typist represents the soul. The typewriter represents the mind and the body through which that soul may operate. The typewritten material represents the interaction of the body and mind actuated by the soul with the environment with which that body and soul come in contact; that is to say, the conduct of the individual. If the typewriter is out of gear, it is impossible for the typist to express meaning in typewritten material. We may regard the "conscience" we have described above as corresponding to the typewriter, recognizing a deeper and ultimate conscience in the typist, so that the more perfect a psychological "conscience" the more truly can the deeper conscience express itself in relation to life. It is our job in this, as in other ways, to make and keep the typewriter as effective and in as good condition as possible.

When we come to deal with the question of love, we must recognize that again our psychological discussion is dealing with factors in the typewriter. It does not deal directly with the deeper things which may exist in the typist of our analogy.

We must now trace out the influence of the three factors of love which have already been mentioned. There is, first of all, the factor described in connection with the protective influence of the father. This is a very important factor in the life of both boys and girls during their early years. In the boy, however, it becomes less and less important as time goes on, and is steadily replaced by a desire for equality with the father with a view to ultimate independence in manhood. In the case of the girl, however, this dependence on the father persists and even develops in the teens, and is ultimately demanded of the husband.

The second factor described, that of dependence

on the mother and retreat to her from reality, should gradually diminish as the child learns to adjust to changes of environment, so that again in adolescence it tends to remain a more important factor in the normal emotional life of the girl than in the case of the boy.

The third factor, that of the normal attraction of the boy to the mother and the girl to the father, normally tends to fall into abeyance between the ages of five and ten. It then reappears, in the boy as a healthy desire to be courteous to his mother and others of her sex, and in the girl as a demand for the companionship of her father and an expression of interest in his hobbies, so that in the normal boy or girl attachment to the parent of the opposite sex is essentially part of the achievement of complete adulthood.

So much for the consideration of psychological mechanisms and their bearing on authority and discipline. We must now consider the practical application of these considerations, and we will assume (1) that the development of the early conscience has been achieved as satisfactorily as possible, and (2) that the sense of unity between the parents and their affection for the child has been fully accepted by it; that love factors are operating in a healthy and open manner; that, as far as possible, the sense of guilt fear has been removed from the child and we have a sound general basis for character development.

We have discussed the various psychological mechanisms of love and fear which must be the basis for authority and discipline, and if we consider for a moment we shall call to mind examples of children who have been ruled too much by fear, of others where sentimentality has been predominant, and others where studied neglect, which has of late been rather the fashion, has been the plan of action. In all these cases the parents have been doing what they believed to be best, in some cases at considerable cost to themselves, in others, gratifying themselves at the cost of their children without realizing it. In all cases the results have fallen short of the parents' desires. The modern tendency to give the child complete freedom of expression regardless of the consequences to itself or others (according to the theory that only along such lines can free personality develop) is not a kind one, nor does it ever achieve its object. The consequences to the child will often be very painful and it may become frightened of life. Again, however much the parents may be prepared to tolerate, when the child comes in contact with other people it will find them less indulgent; it will therefore come to the conclusion that life is unfair and hard, and that its parents have "let it down" by giving it the impression that freedom was permissible. It realizes that it has lacked the guidance and help which the greater experience of the parents might well have provided. The fact is that such treatment encourages the child to express its egocentric desires, without guiding it to a state of development in which it recognizes the rights of others and the value of taking its place in the community. It may be driven either to retreat from the hard world to the refuge of home or to adopt an anti-social attitude towards society.

Nevertheless this tendency to give the child freedom for complete so-called self-expression and development is only the swing of the pendulum from the opposite extreme of over-dominance by fear of the father, or over-anxiety on the part of the doting mother. We are certainly very scathing with regard to other people whom we know we can describe as over-doting or over-strict, but we must be careful not to fall into a similar trap ourselves. It is only too easy to inspire our children with fear through our own over-anxiety and caution, or to get irritable and over-done because our healthy child causes us personal inconveniences. It would perhaps be impossible for any human being to avoid either of these two dangers completely, but we must do our best to achieve perfection in these respects.

How are we to find the middle line which will give children as true a freedom as possible for the development and expression of their own personalities? The home world provides the basis of the development of the child's social adaptability and ideals, and there the predominant factor must be love. The child will respond to this love and will endeavour to please the parents on account of it. In the background, however, there is the substratum of fear, which will be sufficient to reinforce the love motive and so compel the child to react rightly, where the love motive alone would be insufficient. In the early days of the child's life the fear mechanism is important, since the love factor takes time to develop. The value of fear, however, decreases as the love factor gains power, until, on reaching adulthood, fear should have become to all intents and purposes non-existent, while the love factor should spread out into the whole relationship of the individual with the world. The more effectively this has been achieved by the parents, the easier it will be for the child to attain to it itself.

Children must feel a sense of psychological security and an objective attitude in the parents, not only in relation to themselves but in relation to others. It may be said that the small child cannot understand all this, but there is plenty of evidence to show that the child does recall impressions, even though it might not be able to interpret them. Later, it interprets these emotional impressions in the light of its subsequent experience. We must therefore be just as careful in our relationships with the infant as with the older child.

The child is building up each concept of its own ideals on the parents, even though its personal mode of expressing these ideals in later life will depend on its own personality. The first essential is a recognition by the child of the self-sacrificing yet Spartan love on the part of the parents. It will be seen that such an attitude will call forth response from the child along similar lines. This Spartan love, however, will often involve opposing the child's immediate demands for the sake of its future welfare. A recognition of the need for refusing the child's demands is generally due to our own greater experience and knowledge, so we must never treat the child as though it were wicked when it really could not know that what it wanted to do was inadvisable. When the foundation of sound love and security is laid, the child will recognize that what the parents demand of it is demanded in love for its own welfare. There will then be no sense of distrust or antagonism when the parent opposes the child's wishes or deals firmly with it when it is "naughty." It may be said, "Why should the child be naughty under such conditions?" The child has its own personality which is distinct from that of the parents, and in the common course of the development of this personality, demands practice and experience of clash with other personalities. If a child is acting in a way which is obviously "trying it on," and which it is unwise to allow to continue, we can deal with the situation by ignoring the child (except so far as it may be wise to avoid any harm being done by the behaviour). We can give the child the impression, so far as possible, that it does not exist until it has become good again. We must, however, be sure that the naughtiness is not due to irritability with a physical basis, since it is often the earliest sign of incipient illness, and is always a concomitant of over-tiredness or general lowering of health. If penalties have to be imposed, they should as far as possible take the form of natural consequences, and not the imposition of entirely irrelevant drudgery or unpleasant experience.

We have used the word Spartan. It is a very important word. There has been a great tendency of late to make things easy for the child and to forget that without effort nothing can be achieved, knowledge cannot be permanently acquired nor character developed. If we are to see our children take their place in life with independent personalities, we must not be constantly helping them over every stile and lifting them over the muddy places. We must teach them how to do these things themselves, and give them practice until they can, by themselves, overcome obstacles with which they are confronted. We must encourage them with self-confidence born of achievement, so that they may never say, "I will try," but "I am doing it." To illustrate more clearly what is meant by this, let us imagine two men with half an hour to wait before dinner. Each of them has an important letter to write. The first says, "I will try to do it before dinner." Result, two lines finished. The second says, "I will do it before dinner," and it is done and ready for the post.

The word "difficulty" should perhaps be deleted from the dictionary since it is polarised in our minds and indicates something in relation to which we are, to a greater or lesser extent, impotent and hence inferior; it should mean something which is going to call for a pleasurable use of the best we have in us.

CHAPTER IV

THE PLACE OF THE FATHER

It is often said by fathers: "Of course, I do not know anything about children. I leave it all to my wife. Women necessarily know far more about children than do men unless the man happens to have specialized in children." The obviously implied inference is that a father who understands his children must be doing so at the expense of things which should be of far greater importance to a man. On the other hand, one has often come across fathers who have been the salvation of their children through their power of understanding.

The importance of the father in the life of his child is as great as that of the mother. The parts which both the parents have to play, while joint in many ways, are to a very great extent independent. There is the place which the mother must fill and in which the father cannot replace her, and equally there is a part for the father to play in which it is impossible for the mother to replace him. It is true that the mother is the most important person in the child's life during its early years, and that the father's importance increases as the child gets older, but just as the mother never fades out of the picture, so the father has his place from the earliest days of the child's life.

From birth onwards the child is establishing the

place of the father and of the mother in its life, and can only base these fundamental attitudes on the conduct of the parents in relation to itself as well as in relation to each other. At this time, therefore, it is incumbent on the father to negate, to the best of his ability, a sense of undue interference with the child's rights in relation to its mother, and to emphasize the sense of strength expressing itself in love and protection of them both, together with a sense of his unity with the mother in relation to the child. In these last words lie his standing orders. He must co-operate with the mother in learning to understand the baby. He must cheerfully acquiesce in putting the child before himself where the child's rights are concerned. In fact, his love for the child must throughout be objective. He loves the child for what it is and for what it needs, not for what he would like it to be nor for what he would like it to need of him. He must also be careful never to appear to be firm or severe except so far as it will be evident that he is really supporting the wishes and decisions of the mother. This state of affairs, while of extreme importance from the very earliest days of the child's life, must continue for several years. Quite early in the child's life important situations will become evident, varying according to the child's sex, so from this point onwards it will be well to deal separately with the boy and the girl.

Let us start with the boy. Quite soon in the boy's life two important matters will become obvious. One will be the evident recognition of the mother as a refuge from the difficulties of life, and the other the recognition of the father as representing the boy's own objective, and as being the person who could help the boy to achieve manhood. These two opposing tendencies—on the one hand a desire for refuge from life, and on the other hand a desire for the adventure of life—will constantly be alternating in the child's mind. The father must here play his part by being willing to respond to the child's demands on him, and at the same time recognize that the demand for refuge in the mother, which may arise suddenly and cause the child to desert the father for the mother in a manner which would be distinctly rude or hurtful in a grown-up person, is perfectly normal and healthy in the child.

A boy has a normal demand for the mother which will be associated with jealousy of the father's rights and powers in relation to the mother, however ideal the parents' attitude may be. It is perfectly right and normal that during the early years of the child's life there should be times when the father must be prepared to be expelled from the nursery by his son, in order that the boy may have an opportunity for personal contact with his mother alone. If the reactions between the parents are right, this will never involve any consequence other than a greater family unity and affection for the father. As the boy gets older the demand for the father as representing the adventure of life will increase, and the desire for the refuge of the mother should decrease in proportion. In the early days of school life a combination of a sense of refuge and guidance in the handling of the adventure of life will involve the co-operation of both parents. Here it may be pointed out that once the sound relationship has been established with both parents, either parent may be able to represent the other in dealing with the child.

When a boy reaches the age of seven or eight years there is a process of hero-worship of the father which becomes gradually intensified, and from eight or nine to twelve years old it is really strong. During these years the boy's taste for adventure will be growing rapidly, often perhaps outreaching what is socially accepted: torn clothes, forgetting the time, a smashed bicycle, a fall in the river and many other possible misdemeanours present themselves to one's mind. These things, if excessive, may be dealt with by firmness or punishment, but will probably resolve themselves to a more socially accepted norm if the father can enter into the thrill of adventure with his son even in spirit—still better in the flesh. A day of united, unplanned, adventurous roaming by father and son may be very valuable.

If the boy has lost his father it will often be found that at this age he becomes unmanageable from the mother's point of view. One often hears a mother say of her son of nine years or so, "Until six months ago he was a model child, but now I cannot do anything with him." This is a perfectly normal situation, for at this age the boy is demanding the guidance and authority of his father, or at least of a man who can take the place of his father, and he despises petticoat government. As has previously been said, one parent can represent the other, so that if the parental relationship has been ideal, no sign may be detected of this loss of authority on the part of the mother, inasmuch as she represents the father's authority in his absence. It will be found that the boy responds directly to his father more easily than to his mother when both parents are present.

The influence of the mother and father will remain with the boy throughout adolescence, but at the age of twelve or so he will tend to transfer his hero-worship to older boys and later, perhaps, to junior masters or perhaps to some other hero of real life or fiction. He has passed beyond the stage of merely wanting to be a man like his father, and is demanding the expression of his own personality, and not that of his father, in the mode of his adventure in life.

This, then, leads us to a consideration of the father's relationship to his son during his teens. He must certainly not say, "Of course, boys at school lose any respect they have for their fathers and establish new relationships." Any sign of disrespect is really an expression of subservience combined with an endeavour to express the independent personality which is emerging. It is the father's privilege during these years to keep as closely in contact with his son's developing personality as possible. He will recognize and respect the boy's hero-worship of other boys, and the importance of his school world and his experience therein. He will give his son as keen a sense as possible of his desire both to encourage the free development of the boy's own personality and to accept the knowledge and experience of youth from his son, in return for the knowledge and experience of more mature years which he can give. In other words, he is developing a true and intimate "friendship" with his boy which is steadily replacing the dependent father-son relationship of earlier years.

To the girl, her father should not, at any time of her life, represent what she is to be in the adventure of life; rather he should represent what a man should be in relation to the family and home. Thus it is clear that in the case of the girl, even more than in the case of the boy, it is necessary that the father's relationship to the wife and child should be as protective, happy and affectionate as possible, and in all ways he must express in relation to his daughter as great a capacity as possible for understanding her point of view. Any disciplinary measures which may be required must be imposed, as far as the father is concerned, firmly and calmly, with a sense of unimpaired love and understanding. This, of course, also applies to boys, but in the case of girls it is perhaps better that the discipline should be enforced by the mother, except at critical points in the child's life, where the right handling of such matters by the father may be of great value to the girl.

On the whole, then, the father's part with regard to

his daughter during her earliest years consists in the evidence he shows her of his loving, protective relationship to his home, to her mother, and to herself and her brothers and sisters, together with evidence of understanding in relation to herself.

During the girl's early schooldays the part to be played by the father and mother will be the same as in the case of the boy, but it will not be so easy for the father, since he must see difficulties and school life through the girl's eyes, which is not so easy as seeing them through his son's eyes, since he has never had the experience of being a girl himself.

When the girl is in her teens the importance of the father is greatest. It is during these years that she is in special need of understanding. She is going through a period when the deep-seated mysteries of sex, marriage and parenthood are causing mysterious stirrings in her psyche, and the psychological changes which are taking place in her are involving a complete reorientation of her attitude to life. Being no longer a child, but not having the experience of the grown-up, she is in considerable need of guidance and sympathetic understanding. During these years she is in need of the companionship of her father, and it is particularly important that this should not be a condescending companionship on his part. The daughter is demanding, most of all, the sense that her father recognizes her as a real comrade and not as a child. The mysteries of life are largely beyond her own conscious formulation, and even where she is conscious of her own emotions and their meaning she is either unable or unwilling to put them into words. There is a region of this emotional experience which she longs and needs to share. It is in this, as well as in the achievement of a sense of *savoir faire*, that the father may be of the utmost value, and it is here that his previous relationship to his daughter will be of the greatest importance. If he has not understood her and made her aware of this understanding in her early years, he need not hope to understand her nor to be able to help her in the most important ways during her adolescence. She will have formed her estimate of him and of his relationship to her long before her teens.

How, then, is the father who has successfully made his daughter realize his love for her, to deal with the difficult problems of adolescence? As has been said above, he must treat her as a real companion and not just as a child. He must make her realize that he will be glad to let her share his hobbies, his thoughts and his opinions, whenever she is willing and able to do so. Having established this mutual companionship he is in a position to encourage her to talk about her thoughts and views, problems and difficulties, without any sense that he may laugh at her or ridicule what she holds sacred. At the same time he may, by his own understanding, be able to see and interpret even more than she herself is conscious of. By a right use of his insight and understanding he may be able to enlarge the scope of her emotional experience, and by showing that he understands things in her which otherwise she may feel no one could understand, he is able to formulate for her many things which she could not formulate for herself.

It is true that such a perfect relationship between father and daughter is rare, but is not this because many fathers have not realized how much their daughters need them, or if they have realized, have been afraid of the delicacy of such an intimate relationship? It is true also that some mothers may spoil such a relationship by a sense of jealousy of the young girl, inasmuch as their love is subjective rather than objective.

CHAPTER V

THE GROWTH OF THE CHILD

THE beginning of the child's life dates not from birth but from conception, and there are many points concerning this pre-birth period which are of vital importance thereafter.

To give the child its best chance, it must have been wanted, and the parents must have been co-operating to this end at the time of conception. The whole problem of the effect on the child of the conditions of its conception can be summarized in the statement that it is the child which is born by the intention of loving parents who have entered into marriage in its fullest and truest possible way, which is likely to have the best chance from the beginning.

During pregnancy the child is in intimate relation with its mother; its circulation is a continuation of hers, so that she supplies it with all its food and oxygen through the medium of her own blood, which contains the same products when it passes through her child as it does when it passes through herself. These products will include the various secretions of the internal secretory glands. The balance of these glands determines the mother's mood, temperament and physical condition, and conversely the balance is affected by her varying emotional reactions; for example, in the case of fear we have an alteration in the secretion of the suprarenal gland. All such changes will be transmitted to the child as they occur, so the mother's emotional attitude towards pregnancy and childbirth and the coming child, as well as her physical health, are of great importance. Particular difficulties or shocks which she may experience have their bearing on the child, so the environment of the expectant mother should be made mentally, as well as physically, as healthy as possible. Her attitude towards actual childbirth should be one of joy and happiness with an undercurrent of calm courage. The child may be said to be quite as susceptible to the mother's love and character in these ante-natal days as in subsequent childhood.

It is the part of the father and of all others concerned to help the mother in the attainment of this ideal attitude and state of health. Let this be taken as a word of warning concerning those selfish and morbid busybodies who delight in inventing alarming stories of their personal experiences under similar conditions. Morbid conversation about childbirth on the part of so-called friends is the cause of immeasurable suffering, not only for the mother but for the child.

In considering the act of birth we commonly think of the mother at this time, and ignore the feelings of the child, but we should not forget that the process of birth is by no means a passive time in the child's emotional life. Previous to birth it has existed in a world of which it is "king." It is kept warm, it is supplied by its mother with food and oxygen, and it may turn when it will; in fact, within the limits of its experience, it may satisfy its own desires without obstruction.

Then comes birth, an alarming process. At the best it involves a prolonged journey through the maternal passages into an entirely new world, probably associated to some extent with a mild sense of suffocation and pain. In the event of prolonged labour, abnormal position before birth, or such accidents as partial strangulation by the cord, the child's normal experience of birth may be transformed into something much more alarming. Such experiences undoubtedly have more or less serious effects on the child subsequently. For instance, certain cases of asthma in children have definitely been traced to a sense of suffocation in the process of birth, and it is probable that a great many phobias and fears which seem inexplicable at first sight are based on such experiences.

After birth, the child obviously needs rest. It has gone through a great adventure, and the more nearly it can then be returned to a condition corresponding to the world from which it has come, the greater will be its immediate recovery; as soon as possible, therefore, it is restored to a condition of warmth and inactivity. This is necessary quite as much on psychological grounds as it is on physical grounds.

The next thing the child has to learn is how to adapt to the new world into which it has been precipitated. This process of adaptation takes several years to accomplish, and if it has not been accomplished before the child has to go out of the home world into a new world, i.e. the world of school, it is unlikely that the child will ever achieve a really satisfactory adaptation to life.

During the early weeks of life after birth the infant must be trained in its earliest reaction pattern. It must realize that it lives according to a definite and immutable routine. It must receive its feeds regularly. It must be encouraged to develop regularity with regard to the excretory functions, and must discover that if it cries with reason its needs will be attended to, but that it will not be picked up unreasonably. With such training it will probably be found that the baby will sleep the greater part of the day and will wake only for its feeds. In fact, it will develop a habit of routine which will serve as a background for a stable and balanced character, and it will sow the seeds of the realization of a balance between the child's own rights and the rights of others. The ease with which this comes about will vary according to the child and its previous development and temperament. All these may be described as early environmental factors.

The specific character of the particular cell has of course to be considered. What does the child inherit from the parents and immediate ancestors? There is an interesting condition known as haemophilia, which consists of an abnormal tendency to bleed. This tendency is inherited by the boys of a family; their sisters do not suffer from it themselves, but transmit it to their children; again, their sons will suffer from it and their daughters will transmit it to the next generation. This is a condition which is obviously inherited. Similarly, curious physical abnormalities, such as an extra finger on one hand, will "run in a family." There are certain diseases which may be transmitted to the child before birth, if the mother is suffering from them, but such illnesses are no more inherited than is a cold which the child catches from its mother during its childhood. Mental characteristics and tendencies may be inherited. This has been proved by the fact that, in the case of the child which has been removed from the parents in early infancy, it will nevertheless develop mental tendencies and temperament which are similar to those of the parents. On the other hand, it may quite clearly be stated that mental or physical disease is not inherited, though the tendency to such disease may be. If, therefore, we know of the existence in the family history of definite physical diseases such as tuberculosis, we take special precautions to prevent the development of such diseases in our children, by giving them as much fresh air and other special care as possible. In the same way, if we know there has been mental instability in our family history, we take special precautions to avoid undue strains and stresses in our children's lives, with the result that our children may well turn out to be more healthy members of the community than do other children with no such history, brought up without any such care. As we shall see later, the development of a stable and well-adjusted child involves a great deal of sympathetic understanding and observation, without unnecessary interference, on the part of the parent. Our child will stand a far better chance, if we take the trouble to understand it and to adjust its environment when necessary in order that it should get exercise for the development of its personality without undue strain, than will the child whose parents regard it as normal and leave it to fight its own battles and allow it to be exposed to strains and stresses which are beyond its unaided powers to tackle.

Just as a child may inherit external physical characteristics, so it may inherit physical characteristics which are not externally evident, such as those which involve the internal secretory glands. This is evidenced externally by the fact that height and general build are determined essentially by the pituitary gland, and it is evident that there is a tendency to family likeness in height and general build. In the same way, the other internal secretory glands modify characters and temperaments. Without going farther into the question of the inheritance, it will be clear that tendencies of the temperament, character and mind, as well as physical tendencies, may be modified, not only by contacts after birth, but also by pre-natal conditions.

We might assume that there would be a tendency for all the children of one family to be similar in temperament and type, and yet this is obviously not so. On what do these differences depend? True, the original cell from which each of the children develops will differ. In other words, the inherited factors may vary, but it is interesting to compare the type of temperament of each child with the pre-natal environment, and this line of observation is often very suggestive. Let us imagine a family of three children consisting of a *nervous, excitable child*, one which is *calm, stolid and carefree*, and another of an *unduly anxious and worried type*. It may be that we shall find well defined corresponding differences in the pre-natal environment. In the case of the first child there may have been a sense of undue anxiety on the part of the mother concerning pregnancy and childbirth, together with difficulties in the home, and with perhaps alternating anxieties and unexpected successes in the father's business affairs. The pre-natal period of the second child may have been one of calm happiness on the part of the mother, together with a period of steady prosperity in the father's financial affairs, and calm sound friendship on the mother's part. The coming of the third child may have corresponded with a period of serious anxieties concerning the health of the other members of the family, or business difficulties. All these factors will have had their bearing on the temperamental make-up of the children.

As has been previously explained, all that is possible must be done to make the environment of the child during the pre-natal period as satisfactory as possible, but there are unavoidable situations which will add their influence to that of heredity in the newly born child. Hence the difficulties which are encountered amongst children in the early stages of life. At the same time we must not overlook the additional point of the actual process of birth which has already been discussed.

We are therefore faced with many factors which have pre-natal roots, and a realization of this will help us to understand much as the child grows.

Normal growth comes under three headings, namely, Physical, Intellectual, and Emotional. All these are interdependent and have considerable bearing on one another, but it is the emotional development of the child which is the most subtle and delicate problem confronting parents, and the one which is least understood.

We can see how a child is developing physically; we generally know instinctively if it is in good health; we can weigh it and measure it and the doctor can assure us that its organs are in good order. We should know at once if it were ill.

We can also determine its intelligence, that is to say, the inherent intelligence apart from the result of education, or, to put it another way, we can measure capacity apart from knowledge. There are standardized tests which have been applied to several million children, and which are so accurate that, if they are carried out by different observers at different times of the child's life, practically identical results are obtained. Estimated in this way, the average intelligence of the population may be taken to be 100. If the child of ten years passes the tests which would be normal for the child of twelve years, its mental age is entered at twelve years and its Intelligence Quotient at 120. If this child had been tested at the age of five years, its mental age would then have been found to be six years, giving the same Intelligence Quotient of 120. The development of intelligence ends somewhere about the age of sixteen years, though the power to use it and the methods of doing so have no age limit.

When we come to observe the emotional life of the child it is not so obvious how the child is developing, nor have we access to standardized tests as to its development or capacity for development, though we have a basic outline of normal emotional growth as has been discussed in the previous chapters; apart from these basic principles, however, much subtle understanding is required to ensure free, healthy, emotional development.

Different children may need entirely different handling under similar environmental conditions. The child may well be likened to a plant. In the garden are several types of plants, and although all these plants have certain fundamental requirements, such as light, air, soil and water, different types of plants need more specific handling. So it is with children. All children need light, air, nourishment and love, but they need specific understanding also. We do not expect all our plants to flourish with identical handling, yet of late there has been a tendency to consider that if the same is given in the way of healthy surroundings and a good all-round education, this same type of treatment should be equally suited to all children.

But this is not so. Children vary in type quite as much as do plants, and we should be doomed to disappointment in our garden if we imagined that our clematis might turn into a standard rose tree, or our common daisy grow into a tall and stately arum lily. We recognize that our seeds and plants will develop along appointed lines, and that all we can do as gardeners is to see that each type of plant grows as healthily, and produces as abundant and beautiful blossoms, as is possible. This is our function also with regard to our children. We cannot make their personalities different; we can only help these personalities to develop and blossom as freely as possible.

The difference in treatment of various kinds of plants is often extreme; one plant may need severe pruning, another would be killed if pruned at all. One plant cannot show its beauty without support, as for example the sweet pea, whereas another is quite capable of supporting itself and would be damaged by restriction. So it is with children. If we think of discipline in terms of pruning, we find that some children would be killed, metaphorically speaking, by too severe discipline, but at the same time there are many children who require firm discipline, and, what is more, many recognize this fact themselves.

There has been a cult lately of complete freedom of growth; the child is left to find its own way without so-called interference or guidance from an adult; but in many cases this is really cruel and may defeat its own end—namely, the growth of a free personality.

There are types of children who need support, and if this is denied them they cannot flourish. Conversely, if the child is the type that is capable of independence, restriction is hampering and unwise.

Our responsibility, therefore, involves a real understanding of our children and a recognition of the type of their individual personalities, and a giving of the best we know to guide them along right lines to freedom, with a recognition that this does not involve turning them out as copies of ourselves. It is common to find that some members of a family appear to be very much alike in their outlook on life, and it is true, as has been said, that there tend to be family tendencies which do result in family likenesses; but this does not mean that individual members of a family may not have exceedingly different temperaments, and that the development of their individual personalities may not need specific treatment. There are cases where this similarity appears to exist amongst certain members of the family, whereas other members have apparently developed along lines diametrically opposed. In such a case it is probable that the authority of the parents has been over-done. The children are not expressing their own personalities but are reacting obediently to the over-dominant parents, either positively or negatively. The members of the family who are taking the negative line are probably simply in rebellion against their parents, and their reaction is only a negative form of obedience and not true freedom of personality at all.

There is a popular division of types, into introverts and extraverts. The introvert type of person is said to live on reason, to tend to dig deep down and to seek knowledge for its own sake, to be quiet with a tendency to retreat on social occasions. The extravert type is said to live essentially on emotion, to establish ready social contacts, and to spread out over a wide field of interests, so getting to know something about many subjects, but tending not to go deeper into any subject than is necessary for the purpose of establishing social contacts as widely as possible. It is assumed that the average person is a healthy combination of both these types, but the value of this mode of division is by no means certain. It was recently suggested that as a number of children in need of help at a Child Guidance Clinic in America was greater than could be dealt with, it would be a good thing to give extraverts the preference in treatment, since it was to be presumed that the extraverts would be more anxious to achieve a normal adaptation to society than would the introverts, and the results of treatment would therefore be better in the case of extraverts. Experiments were therefore carried out to determine whether a clear diagnosis could be made as to whether a given child were an extravert or an introvert. It was found that a child who was apparently a marked introvert or extravert would react at different times in an entirely opposite way to identical situations, so it was concluded that the attempt to distinguish between introverts and extraverts must be abandoned. It would not appear, therefore, that this definition of types has the fundamental value which it was at one time supposed to have. At the same time, it is certain that we can recognize in general terms the type of child who tends to lead a solitary existence and retreat from society, as opposed to the type of child which, under similar conditions, is popular at school, makes large numbers of friends, and thoroughly enjoys all social occasions. The former type may become a leader in some particular school activity for its own sake rather than with any idea of personal popularity. Other types could also be described, but the important thing is for us to study our own children individually and discover for ourselves in each case just what are the needs of the particular child, and then to act on our discoveries without consideration for our personal comfort.

It may be said that it is easy to determine what kind of plant will grow from a certain seed, and that it is not so easy to determine our type of child. This is true, and so adds fascination to work with children.

CHAPTER VI

THE CHILD'S POINT OF VIEW

ONE of the things which is most difficult for the average adult is to see things from the child's point of view. If we imagine ourselves and our child walking along a curly country lane with hedges on either side, we can see over the hedges; we can see the lane winding ahead of us up the hill; we can see the church in the distance, and the little village; cows on one side and perhaps a plough at work on the other; and many other distant scenes. The child, on the other hand, is too small to see any of this, but its view is equally interesting although totally different. The child will be noticing the flowers on the bank, the little field-mouse, a bumble-bee sucking the honey, the puddles at the side of the road, and so on. However much we want the child to see what we see, it cannot do so unless we ourselves lift it up and show it. We can see both if we want to.

So often in dealing with a child we expect it to see things through adult eyes, quite forgetting that it has taken us many years of growth to be able to see these things ourselves. How often, too, do we get irritated with the importance of detail to the tiny child, not realizing that these details loom large in their own world. This, once one thinks about it, is comparatively easy to see with regard to the tiny child, but the same thing applies right through the child's growth.

There are three factors at work towards this enlargement of vision.

Firstly, the actual growth of intellect or capacity to understand.

Secondly, the accumulation of knowledge, and therefore the equipment to understand, and

Thirdly, experience, or power to relate meaning to things.

Even if the tiny child toddling along the lane could see the cow or the plough, it possibly would not know what they were, and, if told their names, would not understand their functions, so that even as the child acquires words, the concept of the things it is naming is not the same as ours. We realize this fact later when it comes to school life. We know that the average child of six years cannot understand logarithms, however much we explain them, and yet in the moral world, if the child asks "Why?" about something it has been told to do, we may tend to think that it is naughty and ought to understand all that is in our minds. We expect it to know by instinct that it must not scribble on the wall, or experiment with the bath tap and so make a flood. Why should it? This does not mean that it is not to be taught these things, but it does mean that we should not hamper their natural urge to discovery and adventure by imposing on the growing mind a perpetual sense of guilt. The life of the tiny child is one of constant adventure. Every day it learns hundreds of new things. Here again, in order to understand the child's point of view, let us imagine ourselves in a foreign country in which we know nothing of the language or customs. All the time we are learning—trying to fit in, trying to understand—and in so doing we tend to get very tired; so does the child. The perfectly normal, healthy child which has to go about in the bustle of the busy adult life is not naughty because it is whiny and difficult. It is tired, and it is tired not only in the way that we may be, because of the noise and hurry, but because its brain is constantly learning new things.

We do our best to adjust the type of our child's food and the size of its helpings according to its age, and to be careful that it does not get indigestion, and we know that a little good food will help it to grow more healthily than will over-burdening its stomach with large quantities. The child that is overfed often turns against its food. This is not always realized with regard to intellectual food. There is so much that we want our child to learn; we want it to compare well with our friends' children, and so we overload its brain with the food of knowledge which it cannot digest, and the child becomes less keen and less adventurous in its mental attitude towards life. This is a very common cause of so-called laziness.

There is so much to learn and so much to do in the world of to-day, that there is a great danger of over-hurrying our child. With regard to the actual acquirement of knowledge, this must be regulated in a commonsense way, just as its physical diet is, to ensure a normal, healthy, intellectual growth. It is far more important to keep alive a desire for discovery and mental adventure than it is to stuff a child with facts. A realization of this does not only apply to our attitude to school work, but it starts from birth. Most people nowadays accept the fact that a steady routine of four-hourly feeds, plenty of sleep, plenty of fresh air, and an unbroken night, is the best routine for the tiny baby. We are pleased when it smiles and begins to play with things, but we must not over-stimulate it to do this. We are ready to lend it a helping hand when it wants to walk, but we are content to let the child take its own time to learn such things.

A little later on when our child begins to do more for itself, or when there are two children in the family and more work to do, our sins begin. The child tries to put on its own shoes and is slow; we tell it to hurry. We have taken the toddler shopping without a pram and we walk just too quickly for it. In a thousand and one tiny ways we press it just beyond its normal speed. If we stopped to think for a moment of ourselves in a new job, doing new work which we were very anxious to do as well as we could, with our employer telling us all the time to be a little quicker—a little quicker—wouldn't we begin to hate our work and want to avoid it? Does not this apply to the child that does not want to dress itself and does not want to go for a walk?

It may try to do these things, but it becomes slower than ever because of the sense of tensity and incapacity that has been impressed on it by this over-hurry. The things we do well and most willingly and easily are the things we enjoy doing, and the seeds of the power to enjoy achievement are sown in very early years when good habits are made happily and there is no sense of rush.

Often, by a little thoughtful adjustment of routine, children could be given time to dress themselves, while the mother could make a bed or do something else useful rather than stand by watching, getting irritated by the fact that the child fumbled, which it must inevitably do at first, so embarrassing it by a vigilant and critical eye.

The old-fashioned house with its large nursery and often spacious attics and big garden is to the majority nowadays an impossibility, but space is an important factor. The child which lives in a home where there is no room set aside for its use is definitely at a disadvantage. It is surrounded by restrictions which must limit its outlook on life. "Yes," people may say, "but how can we avoid this in modern flat life? We cannot afford to give a room to our child." With a little bit of forethought an almost equal result can be obtained during the pre-school years. Instead of having a polished top to our dining-room table it can be a deal top which can be covered with a cloth in the evenings. We can have a plain whitewashed wall instead of a fancy paper. We can roll the carpet up and put all the untouchables at one end of the room, and at any rate for a number of hours during the day our child can feel free to move in at least three-quarters of the room. Is this asking too much of the parents? Which is more important—our pride of house or the happy growth of our child? Is it not better to do something of this kind than to be constantly distressed by seeing our good things spoilt, or for the child to be constantly hampered by the fear of spoiling good things? Once the child has started school this need is not nearly so great, because the modern schoolroom and playground are so equipped that the child has got room to move and express itself.

It is wrong to allow a child to be a nuisance. It is quite common to hear of the young married couple who, much as they love their child, find the toddler an almost unbearable addition to their home. This space question is one of the factors. If the child has nowhere where it has the right to settle, it does not settle and is a worry, and so the long-suffering but irritated parents try to amuse it in one way or another and are thankful when it is safely asleep. It is not good for grown-ups to play with children too much. It is far better for the child to experiment with its own toys than to have its brain worried by adult conceptions of what it ought to do with its toys. Too much interference by the adult makes the child feel inferior, even to its own toys, because it feels it is expected to do all sorts of elaborate things with them which are out of its power of understanding. It is quite possible to develop at an early stage the power to play alone quietly and happily. If we follow on from the quiet routine of the tiny baby into the toddler stage, instead of giving the child a rattle, giving it some solid bricks with which it can try innumerable experiments without damage or assistance, it will grow from a contented baby, that first of all slept four hours between its feeds and then quietly lay awake and watched the leaves overhead or listened quietly to the happenings around it for four hours, to the toddler that will play alone with a few well-chosen toys and a word of encouragement from time to time, from one meal to the next. Steady routine is as vital for the toddler as it is for the baby, and the emotional pattern developed by this routine will colour the emotional reactions throughout life, so that the child which is allowed to be a nuisance to its mother in the mornings is put to bed in the afternoons in order to get it out of the way, and is a nuisance to its father when he comes home in the evening, is likely to be an exacting person all its life with a grudge against the powers that be.

Routine, however, must not become too fixed a thing. From time to time there must be divisions in it in order that the child may be accustomed to adapting itself to changes. Such modifications of routine, however, should be as far as possible in the form of a treat. It is in this way that the child is prepared to enjoy the variations in life which come with responsibility and adventure. We all know the person who is very efficient in routine work, but in the face of an emergency which interferes with routine is entirely lost.

Another important factor in the peaceful upbringing of the child is that we should think before we say "No" to anything. Once it is decided that "No" is the right answer or prevention is the right line, then nothing should alter the decision. If the mother or father, having said that something was not to be done, goes back on his or her decision because the child cries or whines or pleads, how much more pleading and crying will there be each subsequent time? Eventually, in order to enforce acceptance of authority, really strong measures have to be resorted to. The tiny child of nine or ten months understands "No," and it is in these quite early times that many good habits can be made. The little baby that is allowed to pick and choose with regard to its food, to eat half a piece of bread and butter and then throw it down, and then is allowed to have cake, will be more difficult to train with regard to greed and bad manners later.

A trap that we often fall into in the training of our children is that of asking them to do something because "somebody" will not think well of them if they do not. How often do we catch the words on our lips, "What will Granny think?" or "What will Mrs. So-and-So think if you do not eat your dinner?" On the one hand the child may think it very interesting to find out what Granny does think, so he persists in not eating his dinner, but much worse is it when the child meekly responds to this appeal and so forms its values of right and wrong on the judgment of others rather than on its own understanding. Is not this the development of "All things to all men" attitude that brings about so much difficulty in school life and after?

We must also avoid the trap of over-cautiousness. We must not inspire our children with fear, although we may rightly point out to them that they must not be foolhardy and do things which they know to be dangerous just in order to show off. It is by no means easy to allow the child to do things which, while important to the development of its character, do contain an element of risk, but we must do so or it will never develop the fearlessness which is so essential a part of the equipment for the adventure of life.

We shall find that the child will tend to want to imitate in its own play-life what it sees in the lives of its parents. This imitation of the grown-up will, for example, induce the child to sweep the floor, lay the table, count the spoons, etc., and do all kinds of "work." This "work" will soon take the form of actual acquirement of intellectual knowledge. Advantage may be taken of this to set aside a definite hour or so in the day for "work," and this hour will be looked forward to eagerly by the child, and must be used seriously to aid it in the acquirement of knowledge along self-chosen lines, but with sufficient firmness to ensure retention and concentration.

It will be realized that it is important that the parents should be able to enter into the child's own world, but the child will also appreciate being allowed to enter into the parents' world as far as it is able. It should sometimes be given the opportunity of being with the father and mother when it can take an interest in what the parents are doing. Particularly in the case of the boy, it is of real value to encourage a sense of private understanding between the father and the child in relation to masculine occupations. This will encourage the normal development of the child towards the adult attitude represented by the father in relation to life. It is not only important that the child should pass through its early relationship with its mother to the stage of needing greater companionship of the father, but it is equally important that it should feel that the path is as open as possible on the father's side.

It has often been argued that the child should have everything on a miniature scale to correspond with its size and strength, and should be trained to do such things as laying a table, sweeping a room, and so forth, with such miniature equipment. This is all very well so far as it goes, but it will be found that the normal, healthy child is not satisfied with these things, and will want to move big chairs about, to handle normal sized crockery, and to push a big broom when it gets a chance. Now it is true that we must not allow a child to do things which are really beyond its strength, but at the same time we must not overlook the fact that it is a healthy sign when a child wants to deal with things on the scale in which they exist in the real world. They may be encouraged to get their training in such matters with the miniature equipment, but they must be allowed the satisfaction of demonstrating their capacity for handling such things on a grown-up scale as a reward for efficiency in dealing with things on a small scale. We shall also find that we are amply rewarded if we trust our children to handle breakable things, such as cups and saucers, for they will respond to the confidence, and breakages may well be less frequent in their hands than in the hands of older people.

CHAPTER VII

THE FAMILY CIRCLE

THE baby arrives on its adventure into life, and its adaptation to the new world in which it finds itself is largely affected by its handling in the first week or two. Day by day the baby finds that it receives food from its mother at regular intervals, a daily routine is established, and there is an air of calm efficiency. If it cries on account of pain or for any real reason, it obtains immediate response, but if it cries for any other reason it cannot deceive the powers-that-be. So it passes through the first few weeks.

For the first nine months of life the baby is in intimate relationship with its mother, who refuses to accept any excuse for failing to feed her own child, knowing that this natural provision will have far-reaching effects in the relationship of the child to herself throughout life. It is exceedingly rare to find that the mother's inability to feed her own baby is really due to physical causes. Mental adjustment is a very big factor in this. The experience of running a home for mothers who had difficulty in feeding their new-born babies showed that in no single case was this failure insuperable.

All the happenings in the life of the tiny baby leave indelible marks. We know that in our own lives the first time of doing anything is likely to stand out in relief as compared with the innumerable subsequent times of doing the same thing. To the baby all experiences are inevitably new and so impress their pattern on the child's personality. We must not forget that the child understands long before it has learnt to speak, and that atmosphere is important.

In the previous chapter the gradual emergence from the routine of the baby to the regulated life of the pre-school child was described, but however well we may have regulated this life we are up against inevitable problems if the child is an only child.

What is it that makes one say of a child, "This is an only child"? The parents may be of any type, and yet we have little doubt in our judgment. It is true that some "only children" are less obviously so than others. We find that the less obvious "only child" is one which has been brought up, as far as possible, with playmates, and probably has cousins of its own age with whom it has always been in close contact. Yet even so, there is something by which we can distinguish it from one of a family. It is therefore clear that the existence of brothers and sisters has a great effect, and that the lack of these cannot be compensated for, however much trouble is taken in finding companionship, even though such companionship may be largely that of close relations, such as cousins.

When one considers what it is that we recognize in an "only child" whereby we can label it, we find it is not so much the feeling that the child is spoilt (since the wise parent may be able to handle this problem more or less satisfactorily), but that it is too old for its years, and gives one a sense of its being strained to a much more grown-up outlook than the normal child of its age should possess.

As has already been pointed out, it is impossible for a grown-up person, however much alive to the dangers of the situation, to live and think continuously at the real intellectual and emotional level of a child. Parents may do their utmost to counterbalance the fact that there are no brothers or sisters by obtaining for their child as many playmates of similar age as possible. But this still leaves vacant a great part of the child's life which ought to be occupied by the companionship of other children instead of the parents. Even if another child is introduced into the household as a companion, the fact that the companion is not really a child of the parents gives a sense of inequality, and the inferiority of the second child largely neutralizes the benefit of its presence.

The first child in a family is necessarily an "only child" for a time. If it remains an "only child" for five or more years, it is almost inevitable that it will have permanent traits of the "only child," however many brothers and sisters may subsequently enter the family circle. It is of vital importance that if possible a second child shall be born not more than two or three years after the first. In that case, with suitable handling, the companionship of the second child will be a joy to the first, and this, together with a sense of importance in being the elder child, will far outweigh any sense of loss of the apparent advantages of being the only one and attracting the whole of the parental interest.

The advent of the younger child provides the older child with a companion with whom to play and to whom it can teach games, and someone it can generally patronize and look after. The new situation gives rise to opportunities for unselfishness and thoughtfulness to which the older child will readily respond. At the same time, it will necessarily involve a discipline in the reduction in attention which is given by the grown-ups to the older child, and, to a greater or lesser extent, the compulsory giving up of privileges and small pleasures to the newcomer. Here we begin to get the training which is so important and so difficult to make up for in the case of the only child. This discipline and training is increased by every addition to the nursery world, and helps to develop in the constant daily life those mechanisms and reaction patterns which are to be so important in the later life of the school world and adulthood. It is almost impossible to provide an effective substitute for the interaction of children in the nursery in the case of the only child. However far we may succeed in getting companionship from without, the only child remains an isolated unit; it is either shut out from a group or else included in it as a guest to be humoured or an eccentric to be bullied. In the normal home life the effect of the family unity amongst the children enables them to rub down each other's corners, and to train each other to enter into the outside world of children with a sound reaction pattern already developed. In dealing with the interactions of this nursery world, again it is important to realize that we must allow our children to work out their own problems in their own way. So long as they are handling each other effectively, we must not interfere. We shall find that undue interference may be resented by the very member of the group whom we think we are protecting, and it will certainly be liable to give rise to irritability and bad temper which would never have been developed had we not interfered.

The value of a family is also very great from a moral standpoint. It is difficult for the only child to realize the intricacies of *meum* and *tuum*. After all, nearly everything in its life does belong either to itself or to its parents. So far as other children are concerned, the unwritten laws of host and guest are invoked, and the reactions of various companions to this problem differ enormously. When we have a family of brothers and sisters, each with their own possessions, the problem of *meum* and *tuum* is clearly defined. It must be solved in some way if there is to be any peace in the home, although the nature of this solution is very largely in the guiding hands of the nurse or the parents.

If for some reason or other the first child has reached the age of five years without a brother or a sister, it has already developed the "only child's" attitude to life, and is vastly older than the new baby when it does arrive. The difference in age becomes an unbridgeable chasm for a great many years; in fact, until both the children are grown up. The first child has probably begun school before the second arrives. He has moved on from his first school before the younger one goes to it. This applies, of course, not only to school life but to interests and hobbies, and even privileges in the home life; this gap is even accentuated by the fact that the elder child has very likely developed an abnormally advanced outlook on life.

So far as the younger child is concerned, the difference in age is so great that its chance of entering into the older child's interests sufficiently to gain real companionship is impossible, so the attempt is relinquished and the younger child may be hampered in its normal urge to achievement. When the interval between the first and second child has only been two or three years, the situation is different. The older child is glad to have the companionship of the younger, and it enjoys every effort towards equality. It will be willing in the earlier days to compromise with the younger child in games and other interests, and it will do its best to encourage and teach the little brother or sister, with the result that the younger child will have the stimulus of becoming companionable with the elder. Hence the importance of a reasonably short interval between the first and the second child. The same argument applies, though perhaps not quite so strongly, with regard to subsequent children.

At this point it may be well to mention the unfortunate position of the child which arrives a great many years after its youngest brother or sister. Such a child is essentially an "only child," but with parents presumably well on in years, and therefore less able than they used to be to understand and have patience with the small child. At the same time there will be a group of other people, that is to say, brothers and sisters, who, so far as the small child is concerned, are additional and conflicting parents. Such a child will tend either to be an exceedingly spoilt "only child" or to have a very bad time with a complete uncertainty as to what it may and may not do. In fact, its life will be dependent on the individual characteristics and interactions of its older brothers and sisters, as well as parents who are now by no means able to understand and supply its needs as they were during the childhood of the earlier children.

The character development of the children is also affected by the sex pattern of the family. If the first two children are boys, we tend to get a manly companionship between them; in fact, if the family consists of brothers only, they tend to form manly companionships between themselves. If care is taken from infancy onwards to provide them with girl companions of their own age, they will develop a naturally chivalrous attitude. This growth of natural chivalry is frequently spoilt by suggestion on the part of grown-ups, who take a sentimental and amused view.

Similarly, if the family consists entirely of girls, all will be well if they have the companionship of boys from the beginning and such normal inter-relationships are accepted as being healthy.

It is very common to come across a family consisting of one boy and one girl, the parents feeling that such a state of affairs is neat and psychologically sound. There are points to consider even in such a family, although arguments which apply here will apply with obvious modifications to larger families. If the brother is the elder, there is the natural tendency of the older child to look after the younger, with the additional tendency of the boy to look after the girl. The boy and girl, while finding companionship in each other, will both perhaps need more companionship outside the home than would have been the case had they both been boys or both girls, though in any case such external companionship is important.

In the event of the girl being the elder we are faced with a very definite problem, as the elder child tends to mother her brother and so accentuates the danger of the boy seeking refuge from the hardness of reality when he enters into school life, and to some extent tends to smother the normal instinct of chivalry which every boy should feel in relation to girls. We must be on the look out for danger signals and must do our best to bring about a situation in which the brother, although the younger, looks after his sister when occasion arises, and we must realize that there is very great importance in encouraging relationships with other children in which the boy's natural chivalry may find vent more easily in relation to girls younger than himself.

It must also be remembered that unhealthy sentiment is possible between brothers and sisters, just as it is between boys and girls of different families. It is astonishing how many avoidable difficulties arise through parents refusing to accept this fact.

Much more forethought is given nowadays to the building of the family than was the case when it was more normal to have a family of eight or nine than one or two, and with this forethought various questions arise. For instance, should the number be odd or even? This is not so important a point as some people would suppose, although it is obvious that "two is company and three is none" will necessarily tend to apply, though it is far better to have three children than to have two, but better still, perhaps, to have four. It is sometimes assumed that it is important for the fourth child to arrive soon after the third, in order that the two first may be companions, and the third and fourth may be companions. This sounds well, but it is not always the practical result. In the first place, suppose the first three children are of the same sex and the fourth of the other, it is obvious that the solution of the problem in couples has not been solved, since it is complicated by the difference in sex between the second couple. Apart from this, suppose all the children are boys or girls: it does not by any means follow that the first and second, and third and fourth will be compatible. The question of companionship is far more likely to be dominated by temperamental factors even in early years, and it is not uncommon to find that the first and third, or even the first and fourth children, ultimately prove to be special friends, nor is it uncommon to find that one of the four may be temperamentally so different from the other three that it finds its companionship essentially outside the home circle, and so the problem of "two is company and three is none" arises again! After all, the question of an odd or even number of children is not a very serious one, since in the nursery world the minor problems of life will be fought out however many children there are, and congenial companionship cannot be regarded as dependent on relative ages. In individual cases it will often be found outside the family circle rather than within it.

The essential object of the family group is not the achievement of satisfactory pairing-off, but the discipline and training involved from mere interaction.

It is sometimes said that parents should be companions to their children and should be like brothers and sisters. Up to a point this is quite sound, but it is impossible for grown-ups to avoid some strain on the intelligence of a small child however enthusiastically they may attempt to "come down to its level," as it is perhaps erroneously called. In view of their authority and strength and experience, it is obviously impossible for them to take the place of small brothers and sisters in the discipline and interplay of children. Such a relationship is further prohibited by the subtle emotional relationships between parents and children which have already been discussed. Two children will certainly tend to round off each other's corners, especially if they are children of the same sex, and so they will soon learn to fit in with one another and the difficulties arising between them become negligible. This will be the more effective if the mother and father and other adults are willing to leave the social development of their children as far as possible to the children themselves. Intervention should be rare, but if unavoidable it should be inconspicuous.

In the larger family, however, the more the children the more the corners, and natural adjustment is not likely to take place to the extent of doing away with all difficulties, and a far greater demand for unselfishness is made. The bigger the family the more subtle and unobtrusive can the influence of the parents be made, and the greater will be the effect of the interaction of the children themselves. Clearly, the child which has successfully been brought up as one of a big family is likely, everything else being equal, to make a far better and easier adjustment to school life than will the only child or even the child of a small family. Further, the development of a psychological conscience, which has previously been described, will be far better effected under the conditions of a large family than under those of a small one. In fact, it will be seen on consideration that all the problems of early life will be dealt with better when handled under the natural conditions of the interactions of a group of brothers and sisters than under the far more artificial conditions of a limited world consisting of two children only.

There is an obvious objection which will be raised at this point, and that is that under modern conditions it is not possible to give the best chance to every member of a large family, and it may therefore be unfair to all the children to have more than the parents feel they can afford. This may be true, but we must define what we mean by "the best." In the first place, no amount of money spent on education can make up for the loss of family companionship, and it might rightly be said that it is never fair to limit a family to an only child on financial grounds, and very rarely is it sound to limit it to two. It must also be said that it is not to the advantage of the child to feel that it can get all it wants in the way of educational advantages without personal effort. In fact, it may be enunciated as a general rule that it is the child who realizes that it must achieve its own education and ambitions who does really attain to the satisfaction of its full capacity, and that it is the one who feels that the parents can afford whatever is necessary, who fails to realize the necessity for grit and determination on its own part, and fails to take advantage of what the parents fondly imagine are exceptional opportunities.

We must be careful, in considering the problem of

limiting the family on financial grounds, to be sure that we are not rationalizing, in terms of advantage to the children themselves, what is really the expression of selfish desires for financial security, leisure and other personal advantages.

CHAPTER VIII

THE ADVENTURE INTO SCHOOL

THE age at which this adventure into school is entered upon has grown younger and younger, so that now the question which many parents put to themselves is not whether the child should first go to a kindergarten at the age of five or six or wait until it is old enough to go to a preparatory school, but whether there is an advantage in sending the child to a nursery school at the age of three. This latter idea is prevalent in America, but it is also rapidly increasing in this country. Many boarding schools now cater for the child from three onwards.

Our answer to this question depends on whether we want the school or the home influence to be the stronger in the child, remembering that any influence during the first five years of life has a more fundamental bearing than any subsequent influence, and that therefore this early commencement of school life vastly increases the amount of subsequent influence that the school is going to have over the child. It will have a really complex bearing on the child's psyche, and involves much more than just the question, "Will it increase the child's capacity for mixing with other children or not?"

The satisfactory adaptation of the child to life as a whole is a delicate process: five years is none too long for this without undue emotional strains, and the adventure into school at this age is bound to be a very big emotional event to the child. In fact, there are cases where, with an intelligent and highly strung child who has the opportunity for good teaching at home and has brothers and sisters and also companionship outside the home, it seems wise to postpone the commencement of school until the age of ten, but these of course are rare.

The normal child of under five, however, is not psychologically ready to make much in the way of social contacts with other children outside the home. An observant person going to a children's party will see this. All the small children tend to play happily and contentedly in their own corners, unless interrupted, when there is generally trouble, and it is the five- and six-year-olds who are willing to co-operate and join in social games. So that, if we argue that we shall do wisely to send our child to school at the age of three in order that it may have more companionship, it is a false argument; our reason for so doing must be based on the decision as to whether we feel that the school is definitely better equipped to train our child in its earlier years than are its parents, or our decision may be based on some practical problem arising as, for instance, having to go out to business and having no one suitable with whom to leave the child.

It is far wiser to let the companionship of other children be more gradual, and when the child itself shows a real desire to mix, then is the time for school life to commence. Thus the desire for companionship arises from the child's own need, and is therefore satisfactory and natural. It is no more wise to force the pace of sociability beyond the child's own power of enjoying it than it is to force the pace in any other direction. If the child tends to be unusually anti-social and solitary, then our job is to seek the cause and deal with this, rather than to treat the symptom in ignorance and so exaggerate such a child's over-sensitiveness.

True, there is a strong herd instinct in children, as in us all, and the desires of our children are coloured by the social group in which we live. If the little friends who come in to tea all go to school, then it is probable that our child will want to do likewise and that it will be wise for it to do so; but we must not send it because the others go and we want to be in a line with their parents: we send it because the child itself feels inferior on account of this isolation. Such close similarity of treatment, however, does not arise in the ordinary way, but is somewhat peculiar to such groups as live in garden cities or other communities.

Of course, in overcrowded districts where the problems of bad home accommodation and ignorant or overworked mothers arise, there is no doubt that the nursery school is of inestimable value, and the decision to encourage the sending of children from such homes is honestly based on the desire to increase the more enlightened school influence over the child rather than that of the home.

Most parents who are really thoughtfully desiring the best they can for their children will want home influence to play a larger basic part in their lives than that of the school. The desire for companionship develops normally, just as the desire to walk or talk inevitably develops without pressure from without, and when this makes itself evident, then is the time for school life to begin. It is usual for this social growth to show itself between the ages of four and six.

When a real desire for companionship develops from within and the child starts school, it starts with a further sense of unity and understanding between its parents and itself, because they are supplying it with a self-felt need, and so the adventure into school instead of being a break is a happy extension of home love.

In choosing the school to which we are going to send our child, one of the most important things is to make certain that we can co-operate with the school, and that the teachers will co-operate with us, so that our child will feel a real unity between home authority and that of the school. It has already been pointed out that the authority of the mother tends to get transferred to the father as the child grows older, and that this process is not apparent where the parents are united; a similar situation should exist between the parents and the school to which they send their children. If we find our children are coming up against difficulties in their school life owing to lack of such co-operation on the part of one or other of the teachers, we should regard this as a failure in our relationship with the school. We should take upon ourselves the responsibility of removing this obstacle by getting in touch with the teacher concerned and talking things over.

Let us try to picture the nature of the adventure into school life. In the case of the kindergarten the picture is not so vivid. The whole situation is very similar to an enlargement of the well-managed nursery world. For the girl there is generally an emergence into the higher forms of the same school, and her big adventure only comes if the question of boarding school arises. For the boy the great adventure takes place on entering the preparatory school, even if this is a day school. He will, perhaps, have heard various stories of school life, some favourable and some the reverse, so that we shall be wise if we have prepared him by inspiring him with a spirit of joyous adventure into a world which contains greater possibilities of companionship and increasing knowledge and corporate games. Thus equipped, he will enjoy the adventure of meeting other boys and masters, and of finding his way about in strange rooms, corridors and playgrounds, though he will not be sorry to get back to the rest and security of home. Very soon, however, he will have summed up his masters and know his way about the school, and will settle down to face his real problems in this new life. The problems will essentially be in the interactions with a crowd of other boys of his own age and older, of whom very few, if any, are related to his home life, and many are by no means the type who would have been accepted into his previous home life or chosen as companions for him by his parents. It is here, then, that he gets his first experience of a world which is not dominated by his parents and is not under their control, and it is important that he should not be allowed to feel that they can, or will, interfere with that world unless it is absolutely necessary. The parents want to establish at this point a sense that they are there to help the child to tackle his own problems and to adjust to his own difficulties, but are not there to make life a bed of roses. If our attitude is right, there will be no sense of sneaking, however free the child's confidences may be about other boys, or masters, or his work, since he will know that whatever he tells us the effect will be limited to our advice and guidance as to how to deal with the situation which has arisen.

Let us consider for a moment what are the possible lines of action which a child may take when faced with difficulties at school, and what is the responsibility of the parents in handling such situations. If the relationship between the parents and the child is not one which encourages confidences on the part of the child, it is obvious that a variety of faulty reactions may take place with disastrous results. Such free relationship which makes confidences possible all through childhood days is one of the most valuable aspects of parenthood.

It is not weak of the child to bring its difficulties to its parents. It should find shelter in its home, and a sense of solid security, together with advice and guidance as to its particular problem and any general principles involved, so that it may return to school with a sense of support and the knowledge that it can handle its difficulties effectively. The outcome of this method of helping the child will be that it will soon gain self-confidence and knowledge which will enable it to enjoy its school life and get the most out of it according to its temperament. There are two other methods of handling such situations which are employed by well-meaning parents, but which may lead to serious consequences if the parents, and particularly the mother, are themselves somewhat afraid of life. There is a danger of providing a refuge from the difficulties of the bigger world, so giving the child a sense of a feather bed instead of solid ground to stand upon. In this way they fail to give the child real guidance as to how to handle the problems of its life. Under these circumstances we tend to get the "mother's darling," whose chief object at school is to avoid difficulties and please his mother by being a good boy. On the other hand, the mistake is often made of thinking that our child must stand entirely on its own feet from the beginning, and so refusing a sense of shelter or support. In such a case the child comes up against a blank wall in its home, and finds its school world too hard; it therefore retreats into a phantasy world of its own in which it is able to be pre-eminent, particularly in those things in which in actual fact it is weakest.

For the healthy child who has learnt to adapt successfully during its nursery days, and who enters on the adventure of school life at the right time, and with a sense of the backing of its parents, emotional tangles are not likely to arise. If it is well adapted it recognizes that it can do some things as well as, and perhaps better than, the other children, while there are other things in which it is not nearly so good. It also recognizes that the same remarks would apply equally to almost anybody else in the school, so that it is able to take its part with no undue sense of inferiority, co-ordinating its normal desire for personal power with the application of such power to the welfare of the whole school community. This it will do, not only by use of its own capacities, but also by adjusting to others in the school, according to its judgment of them individually and collectively. Of course, in the early days of school life, the altruistic side of this picture will not be developed to anything like the extent to which it should develop later, but the outcome of this normal attitude towards the school community should be the achievement in adulthood of harmony between a desire for the expression of individual personality, and that of taking one's place in the community to the best advantage of all.

In the case of the child who for some reason or other has failed to adapt successfully to its early environment, school life holds many pitfalls; and the causes of failure to adapt successfully at school, and the variety of reactions to problems, are legion.

Nevertheless there are certain general principles which can be defined and discussed, and which will provide a clue to the nature of the difficulty and its proper handling in any individual case. Failure of adaptation to life necessarily involves a sense of inferiority to others, so that really the big problem we are faced with is that of the sense of inferiority. If we have a sense of certainty that we can do something as well as or better than those around us, we tackle things with enthusiasm and freedom which makes everything easy. If, on the other hand, we feel that people can do something much better than we can, we usually prefer not to do it ourselves; and if we were in a position in which we had to do it, we should not have the same sense of being at our best in so doing.

We have already discussed the question of failure of early adaptation to environment due to psychological difficulties of the first five years of life. There is, however, another exceedingly important cause of the sense of inferiority. In the healthy young child the physical side of life is of vital importance. Hence it is almost unavoidable that the child suffering from a physical deformity or disease, muscular weakness, awkwardness or undersize, will get a sense of inferiority in relation to other children who are not suffering from any physical disability. The effect of this sense of physical inferiority is further increased if on account of ill-health the child's attendance at school is erratic, so that it is constantly having to return to school a comparative stranger. The child which is not endowed with quite as much intelligence as the majority of its class will, by comparison, suffer little during its early years at school if it is good at games and is physically strong and healthy and well developed. In some cases of physical disability, special exercises or other forms of physical treatment may be of considerable value, and it is important that such children should be encouraged to take as active a part in the physical side of school life as is possible. The minimum of emphasis should be placed on any such disability. Cases are by no means uncommon where a child has not been allowed to play games or take other active part in the physical side of school life on account of some doubt as to the condition of its heart. From what has been said, it will be clear that the effects of such treatment, only too often quite unnecessary, may be exceedingly serious. No stone should be left unturned to make quite certain that such treatment is necessary before it is employed. It is so easy to "be on the safe side" physically and not realize that this is very far from "being on the safe side" psychologically. Having done all we can to make sure whether the child really is suffering from a physical disease, and that if so any such disability has been reduced to a minimum, what can we do to avoid the sense of inferiority? This will depend on a great many things. In some cases it may be an indication for home education for some years, during which time the physical weakness may largely be overcome. We may be able to choose a school where the physical factor is not so important as at other schools. Perhaps the child could start school with a group of friends who already appreciate it and so exhibit no sense of superiority. In any case, we can be understanding and can do a great deal by showing that we realize the difficulties which the child is up against. We can openly help it to handle these difficulties in such a way as to compensate for its physical disability by a healthy expression of its character and personality in relation to other children.

The essential effect of the sense of inferiority, whatever its cause, is the demand to compensate by achieving superiority in some other way. This is, *ipso facto*, a self-centred situation, and inasmuch as morality involves a realization of responsibility to others, and a recognition of one's normal part in relation to the whole, we shall recognize that this sense of inferiority with its compensatory demand for power will tend to reduce the child's moral sense and make it selfish and self-centred. We shall not be surprised to find that a great deal of misconduct of greater or less import which we come across in children is due essentially to the sense of inferiority and the compensatory desire for power. It is clear that the earlier we detect the sense of inferiority, and find out as accurately as we can its causes, the better, even though it may involve some hard searching of ourselves.

We can do a great deal to guide children in their demand for the sense of power along lines which are socially acceptable. For example, let us take the case of a little girl who was causing great anxiety by violent outbreaks of temper and threats of violence. This was all due to the mechanism which has just been described, and it was not long before the demand for the sense of power was expressed in triumphant scholastic achievement and her conduct became excellent. In this case there was a combination of good intelligence and a strong urge to power, which was satisfied by intellectual success. It would, of course, be a fallacy to imagine that, because such a child was leading a socially acceptable life as a result of guidance, all danger was past. All that has been achieved is to get the expression of the demand for dominance along lines which are socially acceptable, although the motive is still egocentric. This automatically breaks down certain of the vicious circles involved in the sense of inferiority, and gives time and opportunity to bring the child to realize its value as a social unit, and to teach it, in some cases by open discussion and in others by careful guidance and influence, that this sense of inferiority is a myth, and that the child has a place in life which it can fill as well as anyone else. Its greatest happiness will be in taking its part as a unit in the corporate body of society, and there is no need for it to attempt to achieve a spurious superiority to compensate for an equally spurious sense of inferiority.

CHAPTER IX

ABNORMAL REACTIONS TO A SENSE OF INFERIORITY

WE must realize that although much is said about the sense of inferiority being due to failure of adaptation to life, there is a normal sense of inferiority on the part of the child in relation to adults or older children. This sense calls forth the demand for compensatory power, which demand is healthy. In fact, it is at the root of all ambition and consequent achievement.

So long as the degree of the sense of inferiority is associated with a state of poise in the child's development, all is well. It is only when it gives rise to difficulties which are due to an abnormal sense of inferiority, or when there are obvious causes for its unhealthy development, that we need to regard it as anything but satisfactory.

There are, however, many common unsatisfactory reactions to this sense of inferiority, which may arise to a greater or lesser extent, and which need understanding on the part of the grown-ups if they are to be rightly handled. Such reactions can be divided into three groups.

(1) Direct methods to achieve power.
(2) Retreat into phantasy.
(3) Mother refuge.

It will be found in many cases that a similar mode of conduct may result from two or more of these causes of reactions, but it will be convenient to deal with each type separately.

1. Direct Methods of Achieving Power

(a) *Temper, or other Violent Methods*

Every child is liable to outbreaks of temper which are really an attempt to dominate those in authority, but where such methods are not successful the child usually recognizes the fact and is quite reasonable about it. Too often, however, it discovers that by such means it can get its own way; its parents are afraid it will do itself some harm, or the nurse fears the parents will think she is not kind to the child, or the neighbours may be disturbed by the noise. It is not uncommon for the child to throw itself down in the road in a temper, knowing that it will attract the attention of the passers-by and so will subjugate its nurse. It is evident that, up to a point, the child may be prepared to take more and more serious measures in this direction when its milder ones fail; this is especially the case where punishment, particularly physical punishment, is indulged in.

The handling of these conditions, from the mildest normal temper to the most violent manifestations, should be, in general principle, on the following lines. So long as the child is behaving in this anti-social way it is not worth knowing or bothering about, but, by contrast, it realizes that when it is good it gets into the centre of the picture as a desirable companion. In this way it achieves a normal, healthy and satisfying relationship to its parents and others. If the nature of the outbreak is such that the child may harm itself or others it may be necessary to exercise some restraint, but whatever needs to be done must be done quite calmly and firmly, without conveying any sense that the grown-up is being disturbed by the incident. It will also be found that in many cases when an outbreak of temper or other violence is over, it is possible to have a quiet talk which will help the child to co-operate with the parents. Such a talk must be based on reason, common sense and healthy affection rather than sentimental emotion.

(*b*) *Undue Submissiveness*

A child may realize that temper does not pay in the long run, and so take the opposite line and apparently be extraordinarily good and submissive. This is particularly likely to happen where a child has seen partial failure of outbreaks of temper on the part of another child. This situation is more difficult to deal with, as it is more subtle and far pleasanter for those around. Nevertheless we must realize that this is just as serious and dangerous as are outbreaks of temper: more serious in fact, since we are not forced to deal with the situation. The first thing we must do is to learn to distinguish between the child which has a healthy attitude to life and a sound relationship to its parents and so co-operates with them for the benefit of all, while at the same time it is normally naughty, and the child who is always achieving its own ends by its apparent goodness and submissiveness. It is impossible to give any rules for making such distinction, since it is largely a matter of intuition. All one can do is to urge parents of children who are exceptionally good and submissive to consider seriously whether this conduct is that of the normal, healthy and affectionate child or not. We can often learn a great deal by watching such children when they are playing with others and are not aware of being under adult observation.

In the handling of the unhealthily good and submissive child we are up against a very difficult situation. In the first place, any sense of favouritism in relation to such a child as compared with other children must be avoided, and particularly in comparison with any child which may be subject to outbreaks of temper. In fact, outbreaks of temper should be regarded as suggestive of a finer character than should undue submissiveness and goodness.

(*c*) *Illness*

Apart from unavoidable illnesses, there are many minor ailments which a child can consciously or unconsciously invoke to achieve its own ends. On the whole, these tend to come more under the heading of mother refuge than under the present heading. Nevertheless we must recognize that various conditions—debility, headaches, sore throats, and so forth —may be invoked by the child to achieve power over the parents. "You cannot hit a man when he is down," and illness may cut short a method which is being carried out by parents or teachers and compel the adoption of an entirely different attitude. It is important also to realize that a child may exaggerate the severity or duration of an illness or accident for the same reason.

In the case of the child who is trying to achieve power by means of illness, it may be of value to take the matter seriously and treat the child as though it were really ill, by isolation in bed, light diet, drawn curtains, and so forth. The effects of this treatment will be unpleasant if the child is really well, and so it will speedily recover!

(*d*) *Cheating and Lying*

It is not unusual for a child which has some physical disability, and is trying to compensate for this by success in the intellectual sphere, to find that it cannot get to the top of the class on the strength of its intelligence alone. The urge to power, in such a case, may often be strong enough to induce cheating and lying in order to gain first place in the class and the approbation of the teachers. The applications of lying to the achievement of power are obvious and manifold. In such cases the treatment must obviously involve the treatment of the whole problem of the sense of inferiority, as outlined in the previous chapter.

(*e*) *Getting in with the Wrong Set*

This type of reaction is particularly liable to take place in the case of the boy who feels, and really may be, somewhat effeminate. He has a sense of inferiority to his fellows, both physically and intellectually, or else he does not attempt to compensate intellectually for his feeling of physical inferiority. He finds himself accepted as a ready tool for a group of boys who can so often be found in a school, who are given to anti-social practices of various kinds. They give him a false sense of manliness, since their activities are defiant and adventurous. Such a group of boys will accept him because he is a willing slave, and in due course he will learn more and more of their methods, and may even take his place as a leader amongst them. This type of boy is compensating, more or less successfully, if not morally, for a lack of a sense of manliness.

(*f*) *Apparent Strength and Fearlessness*

This is a no less common type of over-compensation for a sense of inferiority. It may be associated with things which are unsound, as in the group above described, under the heading of "stealing and getting in with the wrong set," but on the other hand the child may be expressing itself as a powerful character along right lines. It is not uncommon to find that children who have a reputation for strength of character and fearlessness are actually suffering from intense fears and anxieties. They may come under the doctor's care for nervous debility, sleep-walking, or other symptoms, when their struggle to maintain their mask of fearlessness in the face of the world has brought them to a state of exhaustion. Such children are sensitive and of fine calibre, but are urgently in need of understanding and support if they are to overcome their underlying sense of inferiority and express their personalities freely without wasteful expenditure of their nervous energy.

(*g*) *Untruthfulness*

A child may intentionally be untruthful in order to achieve its own ends. For example, there is the well-known untruthfulness to avoid punishment, or to achieve a reputation for virtues which have been conspicuous by their absence on some particular occasion. These may be included under the general heading of untruthfulness as one of the methods by which the child tries to get into the centre of the picture. This leads to the appreciation of the form of untruthfulness which many people find it difficult to understand. The child will naturally want to get into the centre of the picture in a way which brings about the approval of those around it. If, however, this proves to be impossible, the urge is so great that the child will be prepared to get into the centre of the picture by conduct, or by statements which give the impression of conduct, which leads to the active disapproval of those around it, since by this means, at least, it is able to attract their attention.

2. Retreat into Phantasy

Retreat into a phantasy world is the second method whereby children may deal with the sense of inferiority. Finding the real world too hard to face, the child may retreat from it into a world of its own. This world may be almost entirely divorced from its actual surroundings, or it may incorporate them to a greater or lesser degree, transforming the fact into fiction so far as is necessary to satisfy the requirements of the phantasy world. It will often be found that such a child, especially in the teens, will alternate between phantasy and reality according to the varying difficulty of the problems which it has to face in the real world. Such cases illustrate particularly well the association of amorality with phantasy. We shall probably find that when such a child is in the stage of facing reality, it is entirely trustworthy and has a perfectly sound moral outlook on life, whereas in the phantasy stage we cannot trust the child farther than we can see it. It has lost its sense of morality at the same moment that it has retired from contact with the real world.

It is extremely important that this association of amorality with phantasy should be realized, as it is the explanation of a great deal of misconduct in children.

(a) *Apparent Backwardness*

A child may have school reports which suggest that its conduct is excellent but that its intelligence is not great. The child may even be regarded by its teachers as the dunce of the school. In any case, it is probably quiet and inoffensive. On investigating the intelligence of such a child, it will often be found that it is well above the average, a fact which the teacher finds difficult to believe. What has happened is that the child has retired from the world of reality and is living entirely in a world of its own; though its eyes may apparently pass over the words of the book, its mind is far away, and it is expending all its energy in a phantasy world. Evidence of this may appear in hobbies in which real capacity is expressed along some line which appears to the parents to be quite useless.

The treatment of such apparent backwardness essentially involves a sympathetic entry into the phantasy world, the door to which may be found in the child's self-chosen occupations, or even in the dreams which it may from time to time recount. It should be said here that the child's dreams should be obtained casually and never asked for except in the most casual manner. This entry into the phantasy world gives the child a sense of sympathy and understanding, and the activities of this world can be linked up with the various subjects of school life, which can be shown to have their bearing on the problems of the phantasy world. Starting from this point it is not difficult to lead the child out of its phantasy world into a realization of greater value and pleasure in its real school world. In such a case it is often necessary, or at least wise, to transfer the child from the school where it has achieved the reputation of backwardness to another school, so it will get a fresh start with teachers who from the first recognize its real capacity. It is often possible, in the course of a few months, for such a child to pass from being a dunce of one school to taking a good position amongst older children than itself in another school.

(*b*) *Misconduct and Stealing*

The question of the association of amorality with phantasy has already been mentioned, but a resulting type of misconduct needs consideration in greater detail. The phantasy world may not entirely absorb the energy which has been left unexpressed in intellectual and physical achievement at school. The superabundant energy may well find expression in eccentricity, or in conduct which, though perfectly rational in relation to the child's phantasy, is anti-social in relation to real life. Such a child may also find expression in the amoral satisfaction of its own instincts and desires without considering its responsibilities in relation to the community. The child which is living in a phantasy world and is therefore out of touch with all sense of responsibility may, as has been explained, tend to persistence of an infantile failure to appreciate the rights of others to their own possessions, and will demand for itself whatever it pleases. So we get a form of stealing which is amoral, not immoral, and which will be cured successfully only by translation of the child from this phantasy world to its real world.

This, of course, is not the only form of stealing which may arise, but it is important to be aware of its existence and to realize its root.

(*c*) *The Solitary Child*

The solitary child is a very evident product of the sense of inferiority. Feeling itself unequal to the task of entering confidently into life with its fellows, such a child retreats into a phantasy world in which it may have ideals and ambitions which are quite in accordance with those of normal, social children, but which it feels it must approach along a road which is independent from that which is being traversed by other children. Such a child often tends to get on well with older people, and may give the impression of being far beyond its years. This is because, instead of entering into the life of other children of its own age, it is all the time striving towards a life in which it hopes to find happiness later. It has always found grown-ups kind and sympathetic and in this respect unlike its ordinary schoolfellows, hence the idea of attainment of adult years will be associated with greater happiness than the present.

(*d*) *Unintentional Untruthfulness*

Intentional lying came under the heading of the desire for power, but it must be recognized that there is also unintentional lying. In the first case the child lies with an object in view; in the second case, in the child's phantasy world, the statements which appear untrue to the outsider may seem perfectly true to the child. The latter variety is, of course, perfectly normal in early childhood, and we accept it in "make-believe" games and similar activities of the child. It is only when we are unaware of the phantasy life which prompts the statement, that there is a real danger of our thinking that the child "told a lie" when it is quite unaware of having done so itself. If the child as a result of a sense of inferiority has entered into a phantasy world at the expense of reality, it will obviously be likely constantly to make statements which, while untrue in relation to facts and hence to what we believe to be the truth, are perfectly true in relation to the child's phantasy world and its interpretation of facts in relation to that world. Such statements must on no account result in punishment, but they can be used as valuable indicators of the nature of the child's phantasy life.

3. Mother Refuge

The third situation which we have to consider is that of mother refuge. In this case the child has retreated from the hardness of life to the refuge of its mother. It has been explained how the mother represents the security of the home. Each of the factors in the child's early life involves this care, and its mother's ministration to its needs and demands provides a safe and comfortable resting-place from the adventure of life and contact with the external world represented by the father.

In any two individuals these two aspects of life may be represented in varying proportions by the two parents, and by others who fulfil their functions in relation to the individual. Mother refuge, therefore, represents a retreat to security and an indulgence of personal desire, to escape from facing and dealing with the adventure of life in the external world. It can be distinguished from escape by means of phantasy by the fact that it involves an effort to achieve escape in actual life.

(*a*) *The Solitary Child*

Again, under the heading of mother refuge, we find the child who seeks solitude to avoid relationship with the external world. During the whole of the time in school it is longing for the time when it can escape to its home again, and instead of finding a refuge in the phantasy world of the future it regresses into the mother-dominated world of babyhood.

(*b*) *Illness*

A child that is afraid of life may do anything in its power to avoid going to school, and will often find that it is easy to achieve this end by minor ailments, chiefly of a subjective nature, such as headaches which it may or may not itself feel to be genuine. But the treatment of such cases of fictitious illness should obviously be different from that of feigned illness with a view to power. Isolation and drawn curtains in the case of the child who is seeking a mother refuge will naturally encourage such a retreat. Parents must recognize that a right degree of sense of shelter is justified and essential, but that the child is equally in need of guidance in relation to its handling of the real world. A recognition on its part that the parents understand the situation but are only prepared to deal with it on sound lines will produce a remarkable change in the child's outlook. It will make it impossible for any such device as imaginary illness to be effective, and so the child will not make the attempt.

(c) *Bedwetting*

This is a very common and distressing disorder of childhood, and is generally a psychological disorder associated with the problem of mother refuge. Before deciding that this is the only cause of bedwetting in a particular case it is important that organic diseases should be excluded by a medical examination. It is also important to make sure that the child is not indulging in bad habits of a sexual nature. These possible causes being excluded or dealt with, we are left with the consideration of the commonest cause.

Bedwetting will usually be found to be due to an unconscious desire to attract the attention of the mother. It is a regression to the age when the excretory functions were amongst the most important things which attracted the mother's attention. It is possible that bedwetting is less likely to occur, other things being equal, where the development of control over the excreta in early life was not taken too seriously, and where, while a reasonable degree of appreciation of success was shown, a wet napkin attracted little if any attention. After all, the child's natural development is towards such control, and there is no need for the mother to lay undue stress upon it.

It will often be found that bedwetting occurs only at times when there are exceptional difficulties to be faced in school life or elsewhere. At the same time it must be realized that bedwetting in the case of a small child may be due to a right demand on the child's part for evidence of the mother's love. The mother must first of all ensure that she is giving the love which is due. Two cases may be described to illustrate the practical side of this problem.

A boy of nine or ten years, who had suffered from bedwetting almost continually throughout life and had been treated unsuccessfully by drugs and other methods, was taken to the psychologist. It was found that he had a sister a little older than himself who mothered him, and that he was turned out of bed every night by his mother who also had all the trouble of dealing with the practical results of his bedwetting. It was advised, *inter alia,* that his sister should not mother him any more, but expect him to look after her. His father was to "turn him out" at night if necessary, and the boy was to deal with the consequences of his bedwetting himself. As little attention as possible was to be paid to the condition, and certain problems in relation to the boy's school life were dealt with. This line of treatment led to very speedy progress.

Another time a small girl was brought to the doctor with a history of bedwetting for the past six months. On enquiring if anything special had happened six months before, the reply was that another child had been born. In this case it was clear that the mother's attention had suddenly been diverted from the little girl to the new baby. The older child responded to this by bedwetting, an unconscious method of trying to attract her mother's attention again. As soon as the mother realized this she was able to adjust her attitude to the little girl and all was well.

The treatment of bedwetting, therefore, can be based on commonsense principles. In the first place, organic disease and possible sex problems must be excluded. This having been done, the question of difficulties in adjustment to life must be sympathetically considered and handled, and a regular and calm routine should be established, involving a healthy and balanced development of both mind and body. It may also be well for the father to continue to wake the child last thing at night for a time, but apart from this, emphasis should not be laid on the actual condition, but if notice has to be taken it should be of an encouraging nature. Everything possible must be done to encourage comradeship with the father rather than retreat to the mother, and if bedwetting does still occur the child itself should be expected to deal as far as possible with the consequences.

(*d*) *The Mother's Darling*

Although we all know how objectionable the "mother's darling" is, and what difficulties he is likely to come up against right through life, he is not an uncommon product of modern civilization, so a few words about him will not be out of place. Suppose the mother herself is maladjusted, and as a consequence tends herself to retreat from life into the security of home and regards the outside world as a hard place. She will naturally sympathize with her child who apparently finds the same thing. Instead of a bond of sympathy between mother and son involving the development of the boy towards manhood, it will tend to find its fullest expression in mutual fear of the world and the growth of a morbid protectiveness on the part of the mother. Having little interest in the outside world, she will tend to exaggerate her interest in, and appreciation of, the juvenile efforts of her child, and will tend to dote on him with the result that he will develop into a typical "mother's darling." Further than this, she will give him the impression that his juvenile efforts are really exceptional, and will show off his parlour tricks to selected groups of acquaintances who out of sheer politeness acquiesce in her opinions. This will lead directly to undue conceit and priggishness on the part of the child, and will remove all incentive to real achievement. He will lack the necessary criticism of his weaknesses and so fail to cultivate that steady application required to overcome them. Hence we get the dilettante.

Quite apart from the ill effects of the nervous mother, there are refuge dangers in educational methods of to-day. There has been a considerable increase in the knowledge and understanding of the needs of children. With this has come the swing of the pendulum from the old excessive discipline to a situation of undue softness. There is an endeavour to simplify every aspect of life and to remove all drudgery from learning; in fact, there is a tendency in many people to hope that an erect and effective backbone can be made out of jelly. Should we not realize that, though it is our duty to understand our children, it is also our duty to encourage them to appreciate the value of the principles involved in a Spartan attitude to life, to encourage in them the romance of bravery, healthy endurance and achievement. From the beginning of its life a child must be accustomed to reasonable discipline and training, endurance and acceptance of facts. It must be trained and helped to realize the joy of the storm as much as of the sunshine.

CHAPTER X

ADOLESCENCE

In the early teens great changes take place in every child. These changes manifest themselves physically, and equally but more subtly, in the emotional sphere. Physically, there is a sudden step forward towards maturity. The child is definitely passing from a miniature stage to a stage where it is capable of marriage and parenthood. This development is a much more difficult and prolonged affair under conditions of our modern civilization than under less civilized conditions. The manifold problems due to the impact of modern civilization on the normal primitive instincts of the individual, with the consequent repressions and necessary sublimation which hinder their direct expression, involve considerable complexity in emotional development during these years.

The creative instinct is the instinct which is most affected by our modern culture, and it is this which is most rapidly coming to maturity during adolescence. It is therefore not surprising that this is a period of considerable difficulty, during which the child needs all the help and guidance it can get in order to arrive at a true and acceptable balance between natural instincts and the requirements of modern civilization. It must be our object to do all in our power to enable our children to pass through this period in such a way that they enter into adulthood with a sound adjustment to life, unafraid, and capable of true idealism; able also to enter into marriage and take their place as parents who will be a stage farther than we ourselves have been in the capacity for guiding and helping their own children.

In considering the boy or girl who is just entering into adolescence, we must realize that the development of the direct sex urge will involve the need for its expression in some form or other, whatever the past experience of the child may have been. The form this expression will take depends to a large extent on previous training and experience, as well as on innate temperament; it will also depend very largely on adult sympathetic understanding during this period. There is little doubt that the attitude of the parents to questions on sex matters in early years will prove an important factor in the degree of confidence and comradeship which the child will be able to extend to its parents in its years of adolescence. One cannot over-emphasize the importance of the development of a sincere, open and sacred relationship between parents and children in these matters from the earliest years of life. Once a false start has been made, complete atonement is impossible.

The important thing to realize about the developing sex instinct in adolescence is that it is a creative instinct, and that its very attributes are socially inacceptable when expressed fully in their direct form other than in courtship and marriage, but that they are of real social value when expressed in normal social life in the form of creative work and hobbies. Further, we must realize that it is unusual for a child to be able to express the whole of its energy in the intellectual sphere. One always holds suspect a boy who at this age becomes immersed in intellectual occupations but has no interest in physical activities. One feels happy about the boy who becomes enthusiastic about his work and his games, and at the same time develops definite and suitable ideas as to his future vocation.

Judgment of a girl during the same period is somewhat similar, though evidence of the development of the maternal instinct in the form of real interest and patience in the handling of young children will often largely take the place of the enthusiasm of the boy for other things, and is in itself a strong indication of the choice of the normal vocation of the woman. Sentimental or emotional relationships with other children of the same or opposite sex must always be regarded as danger-signals, at least until the teens are well advanced; that is to say, until the normal stage of emergence into adulthood is well established. When this has occurred, the handling of the development of emotional relationships between young people of the opposite sex comes into an entirely different category.

In the early years of adolescence, children should be encouraged in their hobbies, work, games and ambitions. Through these, parents or teachers may develop a friendship which enables them to keep in close contact with the problems which may arise at this time.

We shall be well advised to let our children take their part in social activities during adolescence, in order that they may become steadily accustomed to the social expression of their instincts while they are still under guidance, so that later they do not fail to find their feet in social life because they have not had that experience of normal social intercourse which would enable them to get it in a true perspective.

It is the attribute of the man to go out into the world to fight in competition with other men for his home and family, as well as to take his place side by side with others in the establishment of the mutual welfare of the society in which he lives. In games, the boy finds satisfaction for most of these desires. For example, there is expression of the team spirit, the sacrifice of the individual for his side, the strife for personal supremacy and its subordinated strife for the supremacy of his side, well developed in such games as cricket and football. Similar remarks apply to a less extent to such a game as tennis, which gives a further opportunity for the spirit of knight errantry in relation to the partner, and is thus of great value in the the expression of the normal sex instinct in ordinary social life.

It is important to realize as adolescence proceeds that the child tends to find its emotions are outstripping its experience and even its intelligence. It is a dangerous situation and one in which the child needs all the help and understanding that it can get. It will often have strong idealistic ideas at this stage and will be willing to do any social work that is put before it. There is real danger in young people being given as much to do in this direction as they are willing to undertake. In any case, the child is likely to undertake far more than it is physically capable of carrying out. Unless the work is very carefully chosen and carries with it the appreciation of the beauty and calm permanence of life and the wonders of nature, the result is likely to be disastrous. At this stage the child's mind is in a state of chaos; it is trying to find data on which to establish its views on life and the meaning of things, where it really is, what it is, and how it is. The adolescent should first of all get a firm foothold in the world of beauty, wonder, calmness and permanence; more than this will not be managed satisfactorily during the years of emergence from emotional chaos. When this has been done, it will be possible to see in true perspective the harder and less beautiful things in the world. Then is the time to encourage young people to take part in relation to those things without themselves being dragged in the mud or compelled to race hither and thither, never knowing where they are going and thus leading an essentially ineffective life. Encouragement of social service should coincide with the aspect of life which is true and permanent, and knowledge of social service which necessitates contact with the sordid should be very gradual. Emotional shocks, due to conditions about which a child can do nothing, are usually crippling rather than developmental.

Social service which is creative is most valuable, and provides a direct outlet for the growing creative instinct, and develops an attitude of service which is steady and tangible. The more idealistic the parents or the school, the greater the danger of drowning the personality by throwing the child into the sea of life before it is really strong enough to swim. Many children who have developed satisfactorily to the stage of adolescence may be driven back into phantasy or some other form of refuge as a result of too speedy a plunge at this time.

The problem of independent emergence from the home world, with its dependence on the parents, into a bigger world, differs somewhat in the case of boys and girls. The boy during his teens has come through to a stage of hero-worship of older boys and junior masters, as well as others whom he has met or of whom he has read or heard, while at the same time he has remained dominated by the authority of his father or somebody who has taken his father's place. In these ways he has been striving towards the experience of other men which will enable him to model his life to the best of his ability in such a way as to ensure success in the handling of it when he launches out on his own. At the same time, he is still largely subordinated to the judgment and opinions of his parents and those with whom he comes in contact through them, pending a sense of capacity to form his own opinions and act on them. Of course in many ways he has gradually been developing independence of such authority all through his life, but in the later teens should come a psychological rebirth, in which he is born into an entirely new world; that is to say, the world is a new one inasmuch as his attitude towards it is revolutionized. He will come to a point where there will be a sudden awareness of the limitations of the world as he has hitherto seen it, and he will realize the existence of an infinitely larger one. He will have a sudden, active realization of the fact that hitherto he has accepted passively the influence of his parents and the world in which they have lived. His whole environment, teachers, school friends, in fact everything and everybody with whom he has been in contact, have been dependent on the small world in which his parents have enclosed him. He now sees that this is not the whole world and the views of his parents are not the only views held by equally sincere and intelligent people. The world is a vast place filled with things and people of which he has had very little experience. He does realize, however, that there are many really sincere thinking people who do not agree with the views and thoughts which his parents have made him feel are an integral part of the right attitude towards life. The normal reaction at this age is the shedding of the authority of the parents, and a personal, active and independent attitude towards life developed. Parents must therefore expect to find a boy honestly doubting much they hold essential in their own attitude to life, and must be prepared to see him venturing into spheres of thought and action which they feel to be dangerous, and may even feel are wrong.

We may rest assured that if we have fulfilled our functions as parents successfully, and are able to continue to do so in spite of our anxieties, he will emerge into an active attitude towards life which is fundamentally sound even though in detail he may differ from us. The boy who has not come through this phase has not achieved adulthood.

It may be said that the boy's lack of experience will lead him into things which will be harmful, and that it may therefore be necessary for us to maintain that sense of our authority which will prevent him from doing such things. This idea, however, is a fallacy which will hamper him in his future life, or at the best will only cause rebellion and determination to do those very things which we feel are most dangerous for him; whereas if he has accepted us as friends he will talk over such things with us and be more likely to recognize that our experience is greater than his own. Only too often this ideal transition from the authority of the parents to individual independence is hindered by wrong attitudes on the part of parents. We all recognize parents who "will not let their children grow up." They want to hang on to them, and cannot bear the feeling that their children are "leaving them." Sometimes they succeed in this, and as a result we get those pathetic people whose reaction to life is dominated by what mother says or what father says, and who remain dutiful children all their lives. On the other hand, we have a negative reaction. This will take the form of rebellion against the insistent domination of the parents, and the child will apparently hold diametrically opposite views. One says "apparently" because on the slightest investigation these views are found to be based on a strong emotional reaction rather than on fully considered judgment. In such a person's dreams strong evidence may be found not only of conflict with the parents but of a sense of weakness in relation to them and to life in general.

All that has been said as applying to the boy applies equally to the girl, but with slight modifications. Such modifications as are required depend solely on the adult objective of the sexes. The boy is driving towards an independent active attitude towards life in which he must grapple with the problems of society and his relationship thereto, in order that he may safeguard and serve the society in which he lives and establish and protect his own home and family. The girl, on the other hand, is fundamentally driving towards the desire for a mate who has achieved this true adulthood, the bringing into the world of children of her own, and the playing of her part in the service of the society in which she lives, not only directly but through her influence over her husband and children. During her earlier years of adolescence, the girl should find her chief friend in her father. When she reaches the stage of realizing her independence, there comes a stronger realization of other men. Her sense of the size of the world may not be so intense as in the case of her brother, and her religious, emotional rebirth will probably not be so acute an experience.

It is interesting to realize that it is not at all uncommon for a girl to wish she were a boy, though it is by no means common for a boy to wish he were a girl. It is this which is at the back of so many of the sex equality movements. It is perfectly true that our present social conditions are such that it is imperative for every girl to be prepared to go through life without marriage, and without the direct fulfilment of her maternal and conjugal impulses. It is also true that there are a great many girls whose glandular make-up strongly tends towards the masculine type, but on the whole the unmarried woman only finds happiness in so far as in her vocation she is satisfying at least her maternal instinct. It may strike us as paradoxical that so many more women than men appear to be opposed to marriage, or, if married, do not experience the normal desire for expression of the sex instinct. It is interesting to try to trace out the reason for this sense of sex inferiority and for the apparent aversion to the expression of the fundamental natural desires on the part of so many girls. Starting in early childhood, the difference between brothers and sisters is by no means so marked as it becomes in adolescence, but the difference in their treatment is far more marked. The boy is expected to express himself in an open-air life, and to take advantage of half-holidays and any other free times he may get for the expression of his own wishes and pleasures. The girl, however, is often expected to help her mother in the house, in shopping and in various other ways. How often, during a family holiday at the sea, are the brothers packed off to the beach while the girls remain behind to help make the beds and tidy up? In other words, while the boy is allowed to express his own personality comparatively freely, his sister, who at this age has very similar desires to those of her brother, is tied down by activities which are quite alien to her age because she must be brought up to be domesticated! How many girls who would have developed into normal domesticated women have established an antagonism to this side of life as a result of over-training along these lines in early childhood? We can at least understand that the small girl will become jealous of her brother's freedom and will very soon wish she were a boy. This is emphasized by the contempt of the free man for the slave, or rather, the contempt of the brother for his sister, whom he sees enslaved against her will.

In such ways as this are the seeds sown for a sense of sex inferiority. Mass suggestion, economic conditions and the rest, can easily complete the bad work. Fortunately it is by no means every small girl who is so misunderstood, and there are many who, being as free as their brothers to express their own personalities, will voluntarily do so in part by "helping mother" and in part in normal equality with their brothers. What will happen to such a healthy little girl when she reaches puberty? At this age it is probable that deep-seated racial memories play their part. According to the evidence which is best epitomized in the symbolism of fairy tales, the child enters on a period of fear of marriage, with at the same time a pull towards it, which should become transformed into the wonder of romance. We see this in the story of the princess and the frog who induces her to take him home with her and treat him in a way which, while quite satisfactory if he were a handsome husband, is repulsive in the case of the frog. Nevertheless, out of her natural love and pity, she does what the poor thing wants, irrespective of the suffering it must entail on her. The consequence is that she finds out that instead of the repulsive and slimy frog she has a handsome prince, whom she marries and with whom she lives happily ever after.

In primitive days every girl, at the onset of her first monthly period, was removed from her home to undergo certain rites, the essential factors of which were:

1. Teaching as to the direct sex functions in marriage and parenthood.
2. Teaching concerning the duties of the wife in the home.
3. Teaching concerning the duties of the woman in relation to the community.
4. Certain tests of endurance and capacity for bearing pain.

After these rites had been completed the girl was returned to her tribe; in the course of a few days or perhaps weeks, she had passed through the whole transition between childhood and womanhood. In all probability she was forthwith married.

We have no such rites in our civilization nowadays and the girl suffers in consequence. It is not suggested that it would be a good thing to reimpose the ancient rites of puberty, but it would be valuable for parents to accept some of the teaching of these ancient rites, and to act upon it. We must realize that these deep-seated racial memories, combined with definite and speedy changes in the body, will produce an entirely new attitude in the child's mind. This attitude will be associated with a deep-seated fear, a sense of mystery and an inarticulate and intense need for help and understanding. She must not be left to find her way alone and unaided through this uncharted, mysterious and perhaps dangerous country which lies ahead of her. The child must in the first place be prepared in advance for the first monthly period. It is surprising how often one comes across girls who were entirely ignorant of the subject until it came upon them. Under such circumstances the child hardly ever tells anybody about it, and may even hide it up until the second occasion. Not only must the child be warned of this normal experience which is to come upon her, but it must be explained to her as a privilege, being the evidence of her womanhood, which is one of the most wonderful and beautiful things which she will possess. There may be essential precautions required in dealing with it, so she must not be foolhardy with regard to it, but it is not a thing to be in any way afraid of.

Not only must the question of monthly periods be dealt with in this way, but also that of physical development in other ways. Very serious consequences often result from teasing a girl about her physical development at this time. The physical changes which are liable to cause the most serious results if unduly criticized are those connected with sex, such as development of the breasts, but the whole development of the girl into a long-legged, gawky and somewhat clumsy individual inevitably causes a sense of awkwardness and difficulty which will be enormously increased by any attention which is called to it. Teasing along these lines may be an important factor in the causation of refusal of food which sometimes leads to dangerous loss of weight. Less fortunately, because the results are less spectacular, it may lead to serious reactions in the adventure of womanhood which may not be recognized as such until irretrievable damage is done.

We must recognize that throughout this period the girl will need an atmosphere in both her mother and father which will inspire her with the wonder and beauty of womanhood, wifehood and motherhood. Perhaps her father's greatest function at this time is to inspire her with a true ideal of manhood by his own attitude in relation to her and her mother, and by allowing her to have as clear and honest an insight into his own personality as possible, as well as by assisting her in her judgment of boys and men she may meet.

There is another aspect of adolescence in the girl which is almost as important as the one which has just been discussed. This depends on the fact that the period of initiation into the normal reactions of the woman to the community is spread out over a period of several years. During this time the girl is no longer exactly a child. She has left the solid nursery floor behind and has embarked on the journey towards the unknown land of adulthood, not only from the point of view of her deep fundamental instinctive urges, but from the point of view of normal, social relationships. She is constantly faced with new situations, or with situations which would have been easy to solve in nursery days, but which she begins to realize need a different solution from the standpoint of the woman, yet she has no experience of the demands of this situation. When grown-ups include her amongst themselves, they may either insult her by treating her as a child or criticize her because she fails to behave as an adult, a criticism to which a poignant sting is added by her sense of inferiority and intense desire to be accepted as an equal. If, on the other hand, the grown-ups no longer need her and dismiss her from their company, her nursery world to which she must return no longer regards her as belonging to it because she has changed in so many ways, so that here she feels as lonely as amongst grown-ups. It may be that she has at least the company of other girls of her own age, but the trouble is that these girls are liable to be in similar difficulties, and the interaction is likely to be as harmful as helpful. She will not get the aid of adult experience from these girls, and at the best can only get a certain amount of assistance from some girl who shows her that other people's parents can be more understanding than her own!

Such difficulties during adolescence are very common, though they can be avoided. As an illustration, it may be helpful to mention two practical points of the most simple kind which have actually caused great suffering in the life of an adolescent girl. In one case, the girl was allowed to stay up to dinner when there were visitors, but she had to go to bed a quarter of an hour afterwards. She felt this to be intensely *infra dig.*, and would really far rather not have appeared at all. In another case a mother would leave her daughter to choose what dress would be right to wear on any occasion, but the next day would criticize her because she had worn the wrong dress. In neither of these situations did the parents realize in the least the intensity of feeling they excited in the child's mind and which she could not express, though they were really fond of their child and anxious to do the best they could for her. How can we avoid such mistakes? We can make it clear from the beginning of adolescence that we realize that it is going to be a period during which the child will need our help and advice. We can let the child realize that we are sympathetic and understanding. We should as far as possible treat the child as an equal, and let it realize that mistakes it may make through inexperience are generally immaterial and easily adjustable. We must also do our best by sympathetic advice to avoid the danger of the child making mistakes.

CHAPTER XI

SEX KNOWLEDGE IN ADOLESCENCE

It was said previously that nearly all young children ask questions about birth before the age of five or so, and it was pointed out that it is important for such questions to be answered truthfully, although of course they cannot be answered fully at such an early age. After the age of six or seven there is generally a dormant period when sex interest is more or less quiescent, but at adolescence the questions arise again and a fuller explanation is required.

It is frequent for parents to fear undertaking such a talk with their children, and to shelve the responsibility either by ignoring the matter or by deputing someone else, such as a schoolmaster, a clergyman or a doctor to undertake the work for them.

The first course, namely, that of leaving the whole matter to chance, is a very dangerous one, as boys and girls are anxious to find out, but may not have the judgment to go to those who would tell them accurately and satisfactorily.

The result of the second method, namely, that of deputing the work to someone else, however professionally it may be done, cannot be anything like as satisfactory as it is if the parents tackle the question simply and sincerely themselves. Children realize that their parents must know these things. Then why are they unable to pass on this information? It immediately raises a doubt as to the purity of sex. Also, the fact that the parents are unable to share such intimate things in their lives with their own children of necessity makes complete friendship with them impossible.

Another excuse for shelving the responsibility of a sex talk is the fact that the child may learn biology at school, but this does not, and cannot, take the place of an intimate personal talk.

Quite apart, however, from any of these reasons, many parents fail to undertake this very definite parental duty because they feel unequipped for the task, and for this reason it may be helpful to suggest a simple background from which to proceed.

The ideal time at which to tackle the subject is in response to a feeler or a definite question from the child itself, and if one is on intimate terms with one's child such a time is almost sure to arise.

The following outline is not, of course, intended as a bald lesson but must be tempered to each individual case.

"What we call the sex instinct has for its object the reproduction of the species, that is to say in mankind the carrying on of the race, and in particular characteristics of our own family. It is looked at in many ways by different people, but perhaps the best way will be to study the reproductive mechanisms in nature, including mankind.

"When examining water from a pond, under a microscope, we shall find minute jelly-like organisms which contain a small specialized part known as the nucleus. This is the simplest form of life and consists of one cell. All animals and plants are made up of cells which are often set aside for special functions. For example, in the human being there are special cells for digestion, special cells for building up the nerves, others which receive the impression of taste, and so forth. In the amoeba, however, all the functions required for life are satisfied by the one cell. It moves by pushing out processes of itself, forming what are called pseudopodia, since they take the place of feet, and if there is food they proceed in this way until they have surrounded it, and the food can be seen within a small space in the cell. After the amoeba has taken all it needs, it moves on and leaves the residue behind.

"This single-cell animal grows and in due course becomes too big for convenience. At this point we find that it divides into two equal parts, while at the same time a process takes place in the nucleus which also divides, so that two individuals, each with a nucleus, are formed from the one. This is the simplest form of reproduction in nature.

"There is a microscopic pond plant known as Spirogyra, in which we find a single rectangular cell growing and dividing as in the amoeba, but the cells do not separate from one another, so that a long strand consisting of a row of rectangular cells is formed. Sometimes, however, the pond may dry up. When this happens a remarkable occurrence takes place. Two strands come together side by side, so that the cells lie in pairs. The walls of adjacent cells break down and so form a channel between the two cells, and the protoplasmic material from one cell passes into the other and then becomes hard and forms a sort of spore which remains dormant until the pond refills or the wind blows the spore to another pool of water. Then it revives and begins to form another strand of cells by its original method of reproduction.

"Here is found what would appear to be one of the earliest examples of sex, in which the cell which forms the spore represents the female and the other the male. The result, however, is the product of one individual by a complete union of two, with a reduction in the total population!

"Many other fascinating examples of the methods of reproduction in its early development will occur to students of biology, but for our purpose we may come to the consideration of the remarkable process which takes place amongst flowers. Let us picture a flower with its beautiful colouring which attracts the bee. The bee comes to find nectar with which to prepare its food supply of honey. This nectar is secreted at the base of the petals, and so in order to get it the bee has to go right down into the middle of the flower, and so brushes the pollen from the anthers on to its back.

"The pollen of different flowers varies in appearance, and is generally seen to be beautifully formed when examined under the microscope. The bee now flies away to another flower, where the pollen, which it has brought with it from the previous plant, gets rubbed off on to the stigma of the new flower. This pollen finds its way down into the ovary of the second flower and unites with the cells therein to form seeds. When the flower dies it leaves behind the ovary containing the seeds as fruits. There are many ways in which this fruit may be conveyed to the soil, either near by or far away, but in the end the seeds get implanted in the soil and themselves develop into plants with flowers of their own, and so the process goes on.

"Here in this wonderful process is an example of the sex process of reproduction. The pollen, each cell of which constitutes a very small plant, consists of male cells which are conveyed to the female cells of the other plants and unite with them to form single cells, which by multiplication and differentiation in function form in due course new individuals similar to the parent plants.

"A similar process takes place in animals and also in man, but in this case we find individuals of opposite sexes. The male forms cells which are transferred to the female sex organs, in which they unite with sex cells of the female and, just as in the flower, the resultant cell proceeds to multiply and take on special functions until an individual similar to its parents is formed.

"In some cases, at a certain stage of this process, the young one, surrounded with a food supply and a protective external covering, comes from the mother in the form of an egg. In other cases, including that of man, it remains within the mother until it is ready to lead a comparatively independent existence.

"The process of sex growth in mankind is slower than in any other animal. Between the ages of about twelve and fourteen years the evidence of sex maturity appears in girls. There is the development of the breasts and of axiliary and pubic hair. The monthly periods commence, which periods are the evidence of the development of complete womanhood and the capacity for motherhood. Each month a microscopic cell is liberated from the ovary into the abdominal cavity. This cell, in a remarkable manner, finds its way to a tube, the fallopian tube, along which it passes into the uterus and becomes implanted into the wall of this organ. If at the end of a month it has not united with a male cell, the wall of the uterus becomes engorged and there is a flow of blood which washes away this cell and prepares the uterus for the reception of another, and so the process is rhythmically repeated.

"Let us now take the case of the boy. At somewhere about the same age as in the case of the girl, marked developments take place. There is the well-known breaking of the voice and the tendency to take a greater interest in personal appearance. As in the girl, there is development of the axiliary and pubic hair. At the same time there is development of the actual organs of sex, so that sex cells are developed together with certain other secretions, and thus the power of reproductive activity comes to maturity. In the boy's case, however, instead of one cell there are millions of cells available. There is a process in the case of the unmarried male which corresponds in a sense to the menstrual period of girls. At intervals of several weeks, the interval varying greatly according to the degree of open-air exercise, mental work and so on, in which the boy engages, an emission of these cells may take place in sleep. This often gives rise to alarm in the boy's mind, so that care should be taken to make it clear to him that such an occurrence, provided it does not take place too frequently, is perfectly normal and need not give rise to anxiety.

"When sex union takes place the male sex organ forms a channel by which these cells are transferred from the father to the vagina of the mother, the vagina being a cavity into which the uterus opens by a small orifice. The chances against the male cells finding their way into the uterus, particularly to the ovum or the female cell, are comparatively small, but the male cell, or spermatozoan as it is called, seeks the female cell and, if it finds it, unites with it to form a single cell. Once this has happened the monthly periods cease, and this new cell multiplies and gradually forms a mass of cells which, after a time, begin to take on various specific functions and so build themselves up in the form of a baby. At the end of nine months, during which time the circulation of the mother is continuous with that of the developing child, so that she is supplying it with all its requirements, such as oxygen and food and other necessities of its developing life, a baby is born into the world as an independent individual. If all goes well, for some months after birth the child should receive its food supply from the mother's breast.

"It is, of course, obvious that there is no milk available until it is required by the child. During pregnancy changes take place in the breast owing to the development of those cells which will be required to produce the milk. For the first three or four days after the birth of the child, the baby is encouraged to attempt to obtain nourishment at regular intervals whereby it develops the habit of sucking, although at this period it receives a fluid which has certain laxative properties but is not in the nature of a food. As a result, however, of regular suction, a supply of milk is produced three or four days after the birth of the child, and from that time until the child has been transferred to other food, i.e. weaned, there should be a regular and sufficient supply of milk for the needs of the child."

This reproductive process in man is the expression of the creative instinct, which may be regarded as consisting essentially of two main parts: one, the desire for children in the parental instinct, and the other, the actual desire for the physical process involved in sexual union between the father and the mother.

It will be realized that the process from beginning to end is a very wonderful and perfect mechanism for the carrying on of the race. Yet when we look round about us we see how its perverted use constitutes one of the most serious and unpleasant problems with which we are faced. It is as though a very delicate surgical instrument, which when put to its right use may produce the most wonderful results, is handled in such a way as to produce serious and even fatal consequences. These remarks apply essentially to the conjugal instinct rather than the parental. The idea of parenthood is in the minds of most people a pure and wonderful thing, even though they may have had their outlook somewhat marred and restricted by emotional disturbances in their early environment.

All the real problems concerning sex which give rise to the sense of something unclean and undesirable are connected with the perverted use of the conjugal instinct. In childhood there may be sexual stimulation from various causes which may give rise to self-abuse or other faulty reactions to the sex instinct. There is always some sense of guilt in connection with any habit of this kind, even though the child may be quite ignorant of the significance of the habit. In fact, it is not uncommon to find a child who, knowing about sex and parenthood, and suffering from self-abuse, has never connected the two. When such habits or thoughts become conscious to the child as being definitely wrong, one of three things may happen. The child may become the slave of these habits, against a greater or lesser resistance on its own part, and may even become the centre of a group of children who discuss such matters and indulge in sex perversion. On the other hand, it may take the line that such matters must not be talked about and must be pushed out of its mind, in other words, repressed. The results of this latter method may be as disastrous as those of the first-mentioned method. One has only to imagine what would happen if one kept boiling water in a sealed vessel. The third method, and the only right one, is for the child to face the situation and talk it over with someone whom it can trust, realizing that the difficulties arise from the need for expression of the developing sex instinct, which is a wonderful and powerful source of energy in life apart from its direct expression in marriage. By understanding and facing this power within itself, the child will get under control a source of energy which will make it possible for it to achieve its ambitions in life and to get the greatest joy out of living.

CHAPTER XII

VOCATION

It has been said that a man's work should be his hobby. This, as in the case of many other such sayings, contains a great deal of truth, though he should, of course, have other hobbies as recreations. He should find in his work a satisfactory expression of his powers, and for his special gifts of mind, body and environment. At the same time he should have other interests which should also provide physical and intellectual satisfaction, whereby he should use other muscles of the mind and body, while giving a rest to those parts which have been worked hardest in the pursuit of his vocation.

It is interesting to ask the small child what it wants to be when it is grown up.

One of the most satisfactory answers, received from a girl, was that given by a young lady of nine summers, who said that she wanted to be "just an ordinary mother." Of course, in these days girls need to choose alternative vocations to this. In the ordinary way the small girl has her maternal instincts quite strongly developed; she is fond of dolls, of mothering younger children and so forth. When, later, she chooses her life work, or at least a life work which is only likely to be replaced by marriage, we shall find that her choice will be determined along one of three lines. These are:

(1) The expression of the maternal instinct in the form of nursing or teaching, etc.; (2) The satisfaction of the exhibitionist tendency along various lines of public work; or (3) The mere acceptance of a standardized means of earning an income sufficient to make her independent, such as routine office work.

If one asks the small boy what he wants to be when he grows up, one may receive the reply, "a policeman," "an engine driver," or "a road mender." Such replies we shall recognize as being common to the majority of little boys at some period of their existence, and due to the passing hero-worship of a representative of one of these honourable occupations.

In some cases we shall find that the reply involves a much more likely future choice. It may be that the boy expresses a desire to follow in his father's footsteps, in which case we may suspect a hero-worship of the father. Indeed, this is very normal at about the time when the child's age is passing into double figures. On the other hand, the choice of vocation which is a true prophecy of the final choice may be expressed by the very small boy, although it is prompted by no apparent reason, such as hero-worship. It will be found that this choice, though overlooked for short periods in favour of more usual outlets in childhood, is persistently present, if only in the background. In such a case we must beware of attaching undue importance to this expression of desire, or of backing it unduly because of our own personal satisfaction in such a choice. If the parent fastens on to such an early expression of desire, and, as it were, encourages the child to specialize too early, even if only in day-dreams, the child may ultimately enter blindly upon such an occupation and find too late that it has made a great mistake. Alternatively, although the ambition was originally right, rebellion may arise in the adolescent years, and the child who has never been allowed to explore possible avenues freely, will flee from the vocation which would have been right, blindly entering upon some occupation in which its powers are wasted and happiness cannot be found.

It is an important principle that nothing can be done without day-dreams. Crime which is actually committed depends on original day-dreams which have led up to it. However repulsive an act may appear, we shall find that previous images have played an essential part in the genesis of the action. It is therefore important to realize that a choice of vocation depends not only on the particular powers and opportunities of the individual, but on the development of this phantasy life. We must therefore allow the child to develop its own day-dreams and play-life as freely and independently as possible, in order that it may ultimately find its true vocation.

The choice of vocation is one of the most important matters which arise in adolescent years. As will be explained later, there is a danger of a phantastic choice which may prove disastrous. In order to avoid this, we must be careful that side by side with the free development and self-expression of the child's own personality and emotional make-up it also establishes a sound social contact with the world in which it lives and in which it is to take its part. This process must not be pushed, and we must realize that the child's real world during these early years is practically limited to its home, and then to its school together with its home, and the immediate surroundings thereof, and that it is not until later adolescence that the child's world coincides with that which we should find to be our own. We must recognize that our children are individual persons with latent and manifest possibilities and powers, of which we may only very partially be cognisant. We must avoid the danger of too much concentration on any particular power at the expense of general development, realizing that the whole mind and body must have ample opportunity for harmonious development.

It is exceedingly important that mental development should proceed along the widest possible lines, and that all children should have opportunity for a reasonable expression of their natural tendencies and urges in the form of hobbies. At the same time, it is necessary that mental discipline should be employed, not only from the point of view of character development and equipment for adulthood, but also from the point of view of the acquirement of knowledge required in adult life, and of the general cultural development of the mind.

It is this last point which is involved in the view that the child "should not be allowed to specialize too early," and so we have a situation in which an individual spends part of its time at "work" and part at "play." Work represents an organized routine of intellectual and, perhaps, physical occupation, with the force of external authority behind it. The child ought, of course, to be able to feel the value and pleasure of this part of its life. Play, on the other hand, represents the child's own expression of its urges without the imposition of external authority. Play gives opportunity for using parts of the mind which are not used in the course of the child's work—at least, not to the point of tiredness—and so may rightly be called recreation. In the early years this play tends to be occupied largely with the phantasy world, and this is quite healthy. As the child gets older, the phantasy world should diminish and the practical application of the child's vocational tendencies should increase.

So we come to the all-important point that hobbies and play are an essential means of recreation, and so a means of making organized routine work easier, happier and more efficient. On no account must they go beyond the stage of recreation and interfere with the progress of the routine work. This is especially a danger in the adolescent boy. He is approaching the stage where he knows he will have to face reality. He finds himself faced with the problem of examinations, and the difficulty of making a start in life, at a time when his mind is working actively and he is finding much to interest him other than his routine work. He may then tend to enter into his recreations, not only as a means of strengthening himself to carry on with his work but also as a means of escape which he is able to carry with him into working hours. Thus he cuts himself off from reality and exhausts his energy on hobbies instead of expending it on the work necessary to enable him to hold his own successfully in the battle of life. In many cases this situation is so marked that although the boy's hobby might be suitable for his life's work, and although he may have been exceedingly keen on it, his interest goes the moment his hobby is translated into the atmosphere of reality and organized work, under the guidance of authority.

Lack of vocational ambition in an adolescent may be regarded as of serious import. It may arise in the child with a comparatively low intelligence quotient, especially if that child feels sure of security and comfort whether it exerts itself to earn them or not. It may occur in the case of a child whose energies have been used up in any form of mental conflict. And it may also occur where a child is afraid of the adventure of life. The cause of such lack of ambition should be investigated and dealt with.

It does not follow, however, that enthusiasm for some particular vocation necessarily indicates a willingness to face the adventure of life. Nor must we accept such enthusiasm as an indication that the choice is right without making sure of the motives which are at work within the child. We must be certain that there is full knowledge of the various aspects of the vocation chosen, and the preparation involved. It is not at all uncommon for nervous breakdowns to occur in young people either during their training or soon after its completion if they have chosen their vocation on phantastic grounds. Factors which they had not anticipated bring them up against a situation which they are not prepared to face.

How, then, are we to be sure that a chosen vocation is right? Perhaps a boy has always shown an aptitude and liking for a particular vocation. We know perfectly well that he does not even now realize what it will involve. For example, the boy who is keen on being a doctor may have no conception of the work involved in the preparation or practice of this profession. If he is honest he will admit that he felt thrilled when the family doctor came to see him when he was small; he liked the idea of driving about in a comfortable car, scribbling rubbish on a bit of paper and then having another ride in the car. At the same time we may know that he emphasized the hospital side of the army when playing with soldiers. Obviously a vague interest in looking after the wounded soldiers of his toy army, and the expressed pleasure in the idea of driving about in a car all day, and writing rubbish on pieces of paper, is not a sufficient justification for feeling that the boy should enter upon a life which is so fundamentally unlike the picture which he has drawn for himself. Nevertheless we know that for some reason there has been an underlying day-dream which has had the strength to survive all through his early years, and we know, too, that a powerful long-standing day-dream provides the greatest source possible whereby success may be achieved, if the day-dream can be transformed into a reasoned plan of action and carried into practice. We therefore consider the nature of the child's particular gifts and powers in relation to the possible profession of Medicine. If we find that in his school life he has been good at the type of work which is most called for in Medicine, has the social and other attributes which should make a good doctor, and has the intelligence required for a University career, it will still be necessary for him to be shown what entering upon such a career involves in reality. If, after honestly facing the facts which are put before him, he is still as keen as ever, we may happily encourage the boy in his choice, even though it may be at some sacrifice to ourselves.

The importance of sound choice cannot be overestimated. A boy or girl who has chosen a career on false premises, on the one hand, may break down, openly by refusing to carry on with the necessary preparation on the ground of lack of interest, or by the more subtle mechanism of a nervous breakdown. On the other hand, the phantasy motive for the choice may be sufficient for carrying through the training, but may lead to nervous troubles or lack of interest later. At the best it will lead to the work being carried out less satisfactorily, because egocentrically, than would have been the case had the choice been sound.

Before consideration of some phantastic choices, it

must be emphasized that there is no occupation which may not rightly be chosen with perfectly sound motives. The examples which follow may be of help, however, in enabling parents to understand what is happening when a child makes a choice which obviously cannot stand the tests which have been suggested. It is interesting to notice that the principle motivation failures are due to fear of life—and thereby to take warning—for it is in very early days that this fear begins to grow.

It is only possible to deal briefly with some of the phantastic causes for choice of certain types of work. Take, for example, schoolmastering. A boy has succeeded in adjusting happily to his school life and has reached a position of superiority to the majority of other boys, but at the same time fears the bigger world, just as the boy who is leaving his Preparatory School may fear the adventure into Public School life. Such a boy may, and often does, inwardly argue thus: "If I go to college I shall have greater freedom than at school, and yet shall still be in a limited world. Having completed my training and become a schoolmaster, I shall return to the security of school, but shall have the further advantage of being in a more senior position with regard to the other boys." Such a situation is not uncommon, and schoolmasters so produced tend to be popular in the sense of being amiable, senior boys. Occasionally, however, such a master may "have his own back" on the boys, if he himself had a bad time during the earlier part of his school life. In any case it will be seen that such motivation is entirely unsound for the choice of teaching as a vocation. If a boy, having achieved some popularity and apparent success as a schoolmaster under such conditions, adjusts his attitude towards life, it may be possible to transform that which has hitherto been an unsatisfactory vocation into a thoroughly satisfactory one. This adjustment will necessarily involve the acceptance of activities amongst other men outside school hours and, it may be, necessitate entering the business world for a year or two before resuming the rôle of schoolmaster.

Again, take for example the choice of the Church as a career. In this there are two possible ambitions. One boy may feel the pull of pastoral work, another the desire to be a great preacher. In either case one often finds that the picture called up in the boy's mind is that of an easy country life, in which he will be able to do as much or as little as he likes and organize his own time. He will be able to take things easily in the morning, do a little pleasant visiting in the afternoon, and retire to his study in the evening—all the time invested with the authority of the Church. He is, in fact, suffering from fear of the adventure of life, like the schoolmaster described above. He finds his escape in the idea of complete freedom from serious responsibilities, having the power to determine the routine of his daily life just as he likes, all the time carrying with him the external authority of the Church to compensate for a sense of the lack of an individual personality. A young man whose ambition is to be a great preacher may be indicating thereby a strong sense of inferiority combined with a strong exhibitionist tendency. The idea of preaching involves being in a position physically, and so symbolically, above the people whom he is addressing, and of being covered with the mantle of the Church, which is emphasized by the actual robes which he wears. He is thereby speaking with the authority of the Church as a Priest rather than by his own authority as a man amongst men. It is interesting that one often finds that such young men previously wanted to be actors, in which profession, again, we find a strong exhibitionist tendency, and the hiding of the real personality behind the cloak of an assumed one.

Closely related to the Church is the Mission Field. There are many phantastic motives which may induce young people to choose Missionary work as a vocation. It is not uncommon to find that there is a desire to escape from themselves and their own problems, or from the situation from which these problems arise. In practice, it is obviously impossible to escape from self, hence the fallacy of such an attempt. Again, there may be a sense of inferiority, associated with an idea of superiority in relation to the natives of a distant country. There is no field of work in which a saner outlook is more needed, in order to deal with all the problems of adjustment to an environment involving entirely different moral and cultural standards from our own. It is not surprising that the choice of this vocation, based on wrong motives, must almost inevitably lead to a nervous breakdown of some kind.

Another motive which is sometimes found in connection with this vocation is a morbid desire for martyrdom, taking the form in the first instance of a desire for the discomforts of the conditions of the Mission Field, and ultimately perhaps even a desire for death as a Missionary.

The study of matters quite alien to humanity is often the means of escape both from the problems of present-day life, and from personal emotional problems. For instance, the historian is often living in the adventurous days of the past, when such a phantasy world provides satisfaction in bravery and adventure, without any of the real danger which exists in the true adventure of life.

There may also be problems in such apparently simple choices as those of the sea and of flying. It is not at all uncommon for an effeminate boy to want to go to sea, since he thereby feels that he is proving his manhood, because there may be a sense of adventure combined with a sense of retreat in the idea of life at sea. On the one hand the thrill of the life of a rover and on the other hand the comfort of "mothering" by being rocked in the cradle of the deep. Even the idea of adventure is to some extent fictitious, since life on board ship is limited compared to life in the open world.

With regard to flying, this, too, is a fairly common ambition in the boy who is afraid of life. The sense of flight through the air symbolizes phantasy, and is removed from the solid ground of reality.

These are but a few examples to illustrate the dangers which beset us in a judgment of choice of vocation, but it must again be emphasized that these motives will only apply to a small percentage of children. Even when such motives do apply, it will not always follow that change of career is necessary. A change of attitude may be all that is required in many cases. If the child is sincere and a healthy relationship with its parents has previously been established, it will not be difficult to demonstrate the unsuitability of a wrongly motivated choice. Our ground for deciding that the motive is wrong will be discovered not only as a result of direct discussion with the child, but by comparison of this with our previous observation and knowledge. It is obvious that a child whose motives are faulty may in conversation suggest highly satisfactory motives, which, however, are completely inconsistent with our previous knowledge of him or her.

It may be that what has been said will give the impression that the problem is almost an insoluble one, but in practice it will be found that in the vast majority of individual cases it is not by any means difficult to arrive at a fairly correct estimate of the wisdom of a child's choice, provided one approaches it with a mind unbiased by personal prejudice.

Our task is more difficult when a child cannot itself decide on any vocation. Under such circumstances one must form an opinion as wisely as possible, as to the suitability of various occupations according to the child's particular temperament. Opportunity will then need to be given for insight into the various possible types of suitable work, and through such insight and through conversation one must hope to develop a definite urge. A great deal of help may be obtained from the Vocational Guidance Department of the National Institute of Industrial Psychology, which carries out a variety of tests designed to discover particular intellectual and manual capacities and, as far as possible, emotional and social aptitudes. This estimate, combined with knowledge of the various careers, makes it possible for them to suggest vocations suitable to a child's specific requirements.

CHAPTER XIII

INDEPENDENCE

HAVING travelled the course of the child's mind from the beginning, up to the attainment of adulthood, it is a fit conclusion to consider the relationship which should exist between parents and their children when the latter have grown up. This final stage of the journey starts from the point where, if all has gone well, the child should have emerged from the nest and have entered upon an independent life, but so long as the parents are living there is still an inter-relationship which is important.

The biggest difficulty which confronts parents when the time comes for them to lay down the insignia of authority, is the fact that so many people think that independence of their children is synonymous with release from the bond of love. Nothing could be farther from the truth. Love is the one essential bond which should always exist between parents and their sons and daughters, and should outlast all other bonds.

During childhood and adolescence the child is, as it were, in a subordinate position in relation to its mother and father, or parent-substitutes who may have authority over it. It is in need of guidance and help which, when the child is mature, should resolve themselves into friendship, and a sense of comradeship far happier and more satisfactory to parents than any sense of power and authority other than that mutually supplied through the bond of affection. There is no need for us to fear the growing up of our children so long as we are satisfied as to the existence of a fundamental mutual love and understanding in the family, since we shall realize that the comradeship that will exist will replace what we fear we may lose. Our success in the ultimate fulfilment of parenthood will depend on two essential factors: firstly, that we have fulfilled our part rightly throughout the child's early years, and secondly, that we are prepared, not only to acquiesce, but to express heartfelt satisfaction in the fact that the child is no longer bound by our authority. These two factors will ensure that we shall have justified our children in feeling that they want us as their greatest and most trustworthy and understanding friends, and further, that we are quite prepared and anxious to take this place in their life without any sense of authority over them, which we ought not now to possess.

This should be an inspiration to parents to keep pace with them, to learn from them and from others, and so to keep open-minded in their attitude to life in order that they continue to be companionable.

Parents will, let us hope, have the fruits of maturity—the result of the experience which younger people do not possess, also the power of contemplation, a broad and calm view, and many other advantages which increasing age should bring. These should provide much that will be of real value to the young, but only if the older generation is prepared to recognize the value of the enthusiasm of abundant energy, idealism and the desire for experience in youth. There is a danger of jealousy and disappointment of personal achievement on the part of older people which causes them unconsciously to put barriers and difficulties in the path of the young. The will to power may remain a strong factor right through life, and if a sense of impotence arises through lack of opportunity or increasing years, a subtle means for achieving satisfaction is an increased sense of personal importance by the belittling of others. This is a trap into which many parents fall. There are, however, problems of dependence other than psychological which have their bearing on the maintaining of psychological independence. A son for several years may have to be dependent financially on his father, for instance, during his preparation at a University or elsewhere for his future vocation. He may remain in a sense dependent on his father throughout the father's life if he goes into the family business. It may be right under these circumstances that before entering the family business he should have a period in which he is self-supporting in some other firm. Certainly, when he does enter the family business he should receive a salary on exactly the same basis as any other man doing the same work. If in due course he should become a partner, the partnership should be the ideal of what a partnership could be.

Many a young family has its happiness impaired or

even destroyed through the over-dominant father in the business world, and many a business is impaired by the inability of the father as senior partner to know when it is right for him to hand over the responsibility to a younger and more agile mind.

Another method which is frequently employed by parents as a subtle means for maintaining power over their children is in the matter of finance. It is not at all uncommon to find that the parents will be prepared to allow their son or daughter certain sums of money towards the education of the grandchildren or to defray the expense of delicate health, but such sums are in the nature of trusts to be used along certain lines rather than definite gifts to be spent in the way that the younger couple may think wisest.

Undue parental power over a daughter is a still more common vice. How often does the lone mother or father insist either by subtle means or by a direct show of authority that it is the daughter's duty to remain at home? When the daughter is really completely unsuited for the life which they have to offer, and her chances of marriage diminish year by year, she dutifully narrows her personality to fit into the groove which has been fashioned for her. Under such circumstances there is bound to be a restriction of personality and a growing psychological dependence, unless on the other hand a conflict is set up which may eventually result in a severe physical or mental disorder. True, it may for various reasons seem wise and right that the daughter should live at home, but if this is the case the situation has got to be faced very clearly in order to avoid psychological dependence and restriction of personality. The parents, although prepared to accept the companionship and practical help of their daughter, must maintain a real desire that she should express herself freely and as independently as possible in that mutual life. A decision of this kind should involve a severe self-examination as to the nature of the love of the father and mother towards the daughter. Is that love objective or subjective? Are they loving themselves more than their child? It is only if they are satisfied that their love for their daughter is greater than their love for themselves that a right attitude towards her independence can be maintained.

All the way through the parental career the question of objective or subjective love is most vital. Is our love for our children for them as they are, or for them as we should like them to be? Do we want them to be copies of ourselves with opportunities before them which we ourselves have missed, or do we want success for them because of the reflected glory which such success brings? One sees crude examples of subjective parental love, where the child who does badly is disowned, not because banishment is of value to the child, but because dishonour is too painful to the parents. This may be extreme, but in many minor ways there is a grave danger of subjective love. Such subjective love is frequently made manifest by disowning a child who has made a marriage which the parents consider unsatisfactory. The parents, rather than be contaminated by the marriage, will cause their own children to suffer doubly as a result of a possible mistake. It should surely be the sincere desire of all parents that their sons and daughters should marry, even though such marriage may leave the mother or father alone.

Perhaps when it comes to the time of the choice of partner the greatest temptation arises for the parents to step in and reassume the rôle of authority on account of a very real and objective love. Much preparation can be done long before the question of falling in love arises. Free and open discussion on the problem of marriage, and what marriage involves, may do much to prevent a mistaken choice later. When the actual question of engagement arises, certainly it is hoped that if previous relationships have been right the parents will know something. Their opinion may even be asked, but they must not interfere unless they feel sure that there is a very real danger of a mistake being made over this vital decision. Even then, such interference must be in the form of advice, not an attempt at authority. Having given voice to the nature of the doubts which have arisen in order to make sure that marriage is not being entered into blindly, and pointing out such dangers as may be felt are going to wreck future happiness, no more can be done.

Marriage having come about, the new son or daughter-in-law should be accepted on exactly the same terms as has already been described in relation to real sons and daughters. Unity brought about by marriage must be recognized and problems which may arise must be left for solution to the partners of that marriage. They must be accepted as one and their right to independence and need for solitude recognized. If there is a constant desire for parental presence, such a desire should be suspect, since they should have a greater desire for each other's company. They must do what they like with their own children, and advice and help should only be given when asked for, and then never with any imprint of superiority.

Here again much should be done before marriage by free discussion on the problems of parenthood, and if this has been so, in all probability such a discussion will continue when practical problems arise. It is obvious that the methods of each generation will vary, and it is doubtful whether any grandparents have ever wholly approved of the handling of their grandchildren. Nevertheless if we have fulfilled in our younger days the principles of respect for the freed personalities of our children and can feel happy that they are playing their part as parents sincerely, we may well enjoy their children without anxiety, content in the knowledge that they are better equipped than we are to understand how to ensure the true happiness of the next generation.

INDEX

INDEX

For Product Safety Concerns and Information please contact our EU representative GPSR@taylorandfrancis.com Taylor & Francis Verlag GmbH, Kaufingerstraße 24, 80331 München, Germany

Batch number: 10725863

Printed by Printforce, the Netherlands